**"IT'S CERTAIN THAT FINE WOMEN EAT
A CRAZY SALAD WITH THEIR MEAT."**
—William Butler Yeats

"Do you want to marry my son?" the woman asked me. "Yes," I said. "Fine," she said. "Now here's what you do. Always make sure you're on top of him so you won't seem so small."

A Few Words About Breasts

"We have lived through the era when happiness was a warm puppy, and the era when happiness was a dry martini, and now we have come to the era when happiness is 'knowing what your uterus looks like.' "

Vaginal Politics

"Honey," said Bill Blass when asked to explain why his line of cosmetics included a so-called private deodorant, "if there's a part of the human body to exploit you might as well get onto it."

Dealing with the, uh, Problem

CRAZY SALAD

Some Things About Women

by NORA EPHRON

*This low-priced Bantam Book
has been completely reset in a type face
designed for easy reading, and was printed
from new plates. It contains the complete
text of the original hard-cover edition.*
NOT ONE WORD HAS BEEN OMITTED.

CRAZY SALAD: SOME THINGS ABOUT WOMEN
*A Bantam Book | published by arrangement with
Alfred A. Knopf, Inc.*

PRINTING HISTORY

Knopf edition published June 1975
2nd printing .... August 1975
3rd printing .... August 1975
4th printing .... September 1975
5th printing .... September 1975
6th printing .... October 1975
7th printing .... November 1975

Portions of this book have appeared in
ESQUIRE *magazine,* NEW YORK *magazine, and* ROLLING STONE.

Bantam edition published | August 1976

*Grateful acknowledgment is made to The Viking Press, Inc.,
for permission to reprint ten lines of poetry from* The Portable
Dorothy Parker. *Copyright 1926, renewed 1954 by Dorothy
Parker.*

Cover Photo © 1976 Jill Krementz

ISBN 0–553–02815–4

Published simultaneously in the United States and Canada.

Bantam Books are published by Bantam Books, Inc. Its trademark, consisting of the words "Bantam Books" and the por-
trayal of a bantam, is registered in the United States Patent
Office and in other countries. Marca Registrada. Bantam
Books, Inc., 666 Fifth Avenue, New York, New York 10019.

FOR MY SISTERS:

Delia, Hallie, and Amy

It's certain that fine women eat
A crazy salad with their meat
　　　—WILLIAM BUTLER YEATS

Contents

Acknowledgments

I want to thank Susan Edmiston, Rosalind Krauss, Mary Ann Madden, and Jennifer Rogers for the number of times they stayed on the telephone trying to help me figure out what on earth I was getting at; Martha Duffy for suggesting Josie's title; Betty Suyker for her efforts in the opposite direction; the editors of *Esquire* and *New York* magazines for their encouragement and suggestions; my agent Lynn Nesbit; and, most of all, Lee Eisenberg at *Esquire* for being the best magazine editor I have ever worked with.

I would also like to have thanked Josie Davis.

Preface

I began writing a column about women in *Esquire* magazine in 1972. The column was my idea, and I wanted to do it for a couple of specific, self-indulgent reasons and one general reason. Self-indulgent specifics first: I needed an excuse to go to my tenth reunion at Wellesley College, and I was looking for someone to pay my way to the Pillsbury Bake-Off. Beyond that, and in general, it seemed clear that American women were going through some changes; I wanted to write about them and about myself. When I began the column, the women's movement was in a period of great activity, growth, and anger; it is now in a period of consolidation. The same is true for me, and it has something to do with why it has become more and more difficult for me to write about women. Also, I'm afraid, I have run out of things to say.

There are twenty-five articles in this book that glance off and onto the subject of women, and as I go through them, I can think of dozens of others I could have done instead. I don't deal with lesbianism here and, except peripherally, I don't deal with motherhood. Month by month, I took what interested me most, and so I never wrote about a number of things that interested me somewhat: panty hose, tampons, comediennes, the Equal Rights Amendment, Fascinating Womanhood, Bella Abzug, *The Story of O,* the integration of the Little League—I could go on and on. The point here is simply to say that this book is not intended to be any sort of definitive history of women in the early 1970s; it's just some things I wanted to write about.

A Few Words
About Breasts

I have to begin with a few words about androgyny. In grammar school, in the fifth and sixth grades, we were all tyrannized by a rigid set of rules that supposedly determined whether we were boys or girls. The episode in *Huckleberry Finn* where Huck is disguised as a girl and gives himself away by the way he threads a needle and catches a ball—that kind of thing. We learned that the way you sat, crossed your legs, held a cigarette, and looked at your nails—the way you did these things instinctively was absolute proof of your sex. Now obviously most children did not take this literally, but I did. I thought that just one slip, just one incorrect cross of my legs or flick of an imaginary cigarette ash would turn me from whatever I was into the other thing; that would be all it took, really. Even though I was outwardly a girl and had many of the trappings generally associated with girldom—a girl's name, for example, and dresses, my own telephone, an autograph book—I spent the early years of my adolescence absolutely certain that I might at any point gum it up. I did not feel at all like a girl. I was boyish. I was athletic, ambitious, outspoken, competitive, noisy, rambunctious. I had scabs on my knees and my socks slid into my loafers and I could throw a football. I wanted desperately not to be that way, not to be a mixture of both things, but instead just one, a girl, a definite in-

1

disputable girl. As soft and as pink as a nursery. And nothing would do that for me, I felt, but breasts.

I was about six months younger than everyone else in my class, and so for about six months after it began, for six months after my friends had begun to develop (that was the word we used, develop), I was not particularly worried. I would sit in the bathtub and look down at my breasts and know that any day now, any second now, they would start growing like everyone else's. They didn't. "I want to buy a bra," I said to my mother one night. "What for?" she said. My mother was really hateful about bras, and by the time my third sister had gotten to the point where she was ready to want one, my mother had worked the whole business into a comedy routine. "Why not use a Band-Aid instead?" she would say. It was a source of great pride to my mother that she had never even had to wear a brassiere until she had her fourth child, and then only because her gynecologist made her. It was incomprehensible to me that anyone could ever be proud of something like that. It was the 1950s, for God's sake. Jane Russell. Cashmere sweaters. Couldn't my mother see that? *"I am too old to wear an undershirt."* Screaming. Weeping. Shouting. "Then don't wear an undershirt," said my mother. "But I want to buy a bra." "What for?"

I suppose that for most girls, breasts, brassieres, that entire thing, has more trauma, more to do with the coming of adolescence, with becoming a woman, than anything else. Certainly more than getting your period, although that, too, was traumatic, symbolic. But you could see breasts; they were there; they were visible. Whereas a girl could claim to have her period for months before she actually got it and nobody would ever know the difference. Which is exactly what I did. All you had to do was make a great fuss over having enough nickels for the Kotex machine and walk around clutching your stomach and moaning for three to five days a month about The Curse and you could

convince anybody. There is a school of thought somewhere in the women's lib/women's mag/gynecology establishment that claims that menstrual cramps are purely
psychological, and I lean toward it. Not that I didn't
have them finally. Agonizing cramps, heating-pad
cramps, go-down-to-the-school-nurse-and-lie-on-the-cot
cramps. But, unlike any pain I had ever suffered, I
adored the pain of cramps, welcomed it, wallowed in it,
bragged about it. "I can't go. I have cramps." "I can't
do that. I have cramps." And most of all, gigglingly,
blushingly: "I can't swim. I have cramps." Nobody ever
used the hard-core word. Menstruation. God, what an
awful word. Never that. "I have cramps."

The morning I first got my period, I went into my
mother's bedroom to tell her. And my mother, my
utterly-hateful-about-bras mother, burst into tears. It
was really a lovely moment, and I remember it so clearly not just because it was one of the two times I ever
saw my mother cry on my account (the other was when
I was caught being a six-year-old kleptomaniac), but
also because the incident did not mean to me what it
meant to her. Her little girl, her firstborn, had finally
become a woman. That was what she was crying about.
My reaction to the event, however, was that I might
well be a woman in some scientific, textbook sense
(and could at least stop faking every month and stop
wasting all those nickels). But in another sense—in a
visible sense—I was as androgynous and as liable to
tip over into boyhood as ever.

I started with a 28 AA bra. I don't think they made
them any smaller in those days, although I gather that
now you can buy bras for five-year-olds that don't have
any cups whatsoever in them; trainer bras they are
called. My first brassiere came from Robinson's Department Store in Beverly Hills. I went there alone, shaking, positive they would look me over and smile and tell
me to come back next year. An actual fitter took me
into the dressing room and stood over me while I took

off my blouse and tried the first one on. The little puffs stood out on my chest. "Lean over," said the fitter. (To this day, I am not sure what fitters in bra departments do except to tell you to lean over.) I leaned over, with the fleeting hope that my breasts would miraculously fall out of my body and into the puffs. Nothing.

"Don't worry about it," said my friend Libby some months later, when things had not improved. "You'll get them after you're married."

"What are you talking about?" I said.

"When you get married," Libby explained, "your husband will touch your breasts and rub them and kiss them and they'll grow."

That was the killer. Necking I could deal with. Intercourse I could deal with. But it had never crossed my mind that a man was going to touch my breasts, that breasts had something to do with all that, petting, my God, they never mentioned petting in my little sex manual about the fertilization of the ovum. I became dizzy. For I knew instantly—as naïve as I had been only a moment before—that only part of what she was saying was true: the touching, rubbing, kissing part, not the growing part. And I knew that no one would ever want to marry me. I had no breasts. I would never have breasts.

My best friend in school was Diana Raskob. She lived a block from me in a house full of wonders. English muffins, for instance. The Raskobs were the first people in Beverly Hills to have English muffins for breakfast. They also had an apricot tree in the back, and a badminton court, and a subscription to *Seventeen* magazine, and hundreds of games, like Sorry and Parcheesi and Treasure Hunt and Anagrams. Diana and I spent three or four afternoons a week in their den reading and playing and eating. Diana's mother's kitchen was full of the most colossal assortment of junk food I have ever been exposed to. My house was full of apples and peaches and milk and homemade chocolate-chip cookies—which were nice, and good for you, but-not-right-before-dinner-or-you'll-spoil-your-appetite. Diana's house had nothing in it that was good for you, and what's more, you could stuff it in right up until dinner and nobody cared. Bar-B-Q potato chips (they were the first in them, too), giant bottles of ginger ale, fresh popcorn with melted butter, hot fudge sauce on Baskin-Robbins jamoca ice cream, powdered-sugar doughnuts from Van de Kamp's. Diana and I had been best friends since we were seven; we were about equally popular in school (which is to say, not particularly), we had about the same success with boys (extremely intermittent), and we looked much the same. Dark. Tall. Gangly.

It is September, just before school begins. I am eleven years old, about to enter the seventh grade, and Diana and I have not seen each other all summer. I have been to camp and she has been somewhere like Banff with her parents. We are meeting, as we often do, on the street midway between our two houses, and we will walk back to Diana's and eat junk and talk about what has happened to each of us that summer. I am walking down Walden Drive in my jeans and my father's shirt hanging out and my old red loafers with the socks falling into them and coming toward me is . . . I take a deep breath . . . a young woman. Diana. Her hair is curled and she has a waist and hips and a bust and she is wearing a straight skirt, an article of clothing I have been repeatedly told I will be unable to wear until I have the hips to hold it up. My jaw drops, and suddenly I am crying, crying hysterically, can't catch my breath sobbing. My best friend has betrayed me. She has gone ahead without me and done it. She has shaped up.

Here are some things I did to help:
Bought a Mark Eden Bust Developer.

Slept on my back for four years.

Splashed cold water on them every night because some French actress said in *Life* magazine that that was what *she* did for her perfect bustline.

Ultimately, I resigned myself to a bad toss and began to wear padded bras. I think about them now, think about all those years in high school I went around in them, my three padded bras, every single one of them with different-sized breasts. Each time I changed bras I changed sizes: one week nice perky but not too obtrusive breasts, the next medium-sized slightly pointy ones, the next week knockers, true knockers; all the time, whatever size I was, carrying around this rubberized appendage on my chest that occasionally crashed into a wall and was poked inward and had to be poked outward—I think about all that and wonder how anyone kept a straight face through it. My parents, who normally had no restraints about needling me— why did they say nothing as they watched my chest go up and down? My friends, who would periodically inspect my breasts for signs of growth and reassure me— why didn't they at least counsel consistency?

And the bathing suits. I die when I think about the bathing suits. That was the era when you could lay an uninhabited bathing suit on the beach and someone would make a pass at it. I would put one on, an absurd swimsuit with its enormous bust built into it, the bones from the suit stabbing me in the rib cage and leaving little red welts on my body, and there I would be, my chest plunging straight downward absolutely vertically from my collarbone to the top of my suit and then suddenly, wham, out came all that padding and material and wiring absolutely horizontally.

Buster Klepper was the first boy who ever touched them. He was my boyfriend my senior year of high school. There is a picture of him in my high-school yearbook that makes him look quite attractive in a

Jewish, horn-rimmed-glasses sort of way, but the picture does not show the pimples, which were air-brushed out, or the dumbness. Well, that isn't really fair. He wasn't dumb. He just wasn't terribly bright. His mother refused to accept it, refused to accept the relentlessly average report cards, refused to deal with her son's inevitable destiny in some junior college or other. "He was tested," she would say to me, apropos of nothing, "and it came out a hundred and forty-five. That's near-genius." Had the word "underachiever" been coined, she probably would have lobbed that one at me, too. Anyway, Buster was really very sweet—which is, I know, damning with faint praise, but there it is. I was the editor of the front page of the high-school newspaper and he was editor of the back page; we had to work together, side by side, in the print shop, and that was how it started. On our first date, we went to see *April Love,* starring Pat Boone. Then we started going together. Buster had a green coupe, a 1950 Ford with an engine he had hand-chromed until it shone, dazzled, reflected the image of anyone who looked into it, anyone usually being Buster polishing it or the gas-station attendants he constantly asked to check the oil in order for them to be overwhelmed by the sparkle on the valves. The car also had a boot stretched over the back seat for reasons I never understood; hanging from the rearview mirror, as was the custom, was a pair of angora dice. A previous girl friend named Solange, who was famous throughout Beverly Hills High School for having no pigment in her right eyebrow, had knitted them for him. Buster and I would ride around town, the two of us seated to the left of the steering wheel. I would shift gears. It was nice.

There was necking. Terrific necking. First in the car, overlooking Los Angeles from what is now the Trousdale Estates. Then on the bed of his parents' cabana at Ocean House. Incredibly wonderful, frustrating necking, I loved it, really, but no further than necking, please don't, please, because there I was absolutely terrified of the general implications of going-a-step-further with a near-dummy and also terrified of his finding out there was next to nothing there (which he knew, of course; he wasn't that dumb).

I broke up with him at one point. I think we were apart for about two weeks. At the end of that time, I drove down to see a friend at a boarding school in Palos Verdes Estates and a disc jockey played "April Love" on the radio four times during the trip. I took it as a sign. I drove straight back to Griffith Park to a golf tournament Buster was playing in (he was the sixth-seeded teen-age golf player in southern California) and presented myself back to him on the green of the 18th hole. It was all very dramatic. That night we went to a drive-in and I let him get his hand under my protuberances and onto my breasts. He really didn't seem to mind at all.

"Do you want to marry my son?" the woman asked me.

"Yes," I said.

I was nineteen years old, a virgin, going with this woman's son, this big strange woman who was married to a Lutheran minister in New Hampshire and pretended she was gentile and had this son, by her first husband, this total fool of a son who ran the hero-sandwich concession at Harvard Business School and whom for one moment one December in New Hampshire I said—as much out of politeness as anything else —that I wanted to marry.

"Fine," she said. "Now, here's what you do. Always make sure you're on top of him so you won't seem so small. My bust is very large, you see, so I always lie on my back to make it look smaller, but you'll have to be on top most of the time."

I nodded. "Thank you," I said.

"I have a book for you to read," she went on. "Take it with you when you leave. Keep it." She went to the

*bookshelf, found it, and gave it to me. It was a book on
frigidity.*

"Thank you," I said.

That is a true story. Everything in this article is a
true story, but I feel I have to point out that that story
in particular is true. It happened on December 30,
1960. I think about it often. When it first happened, I
naturally assumed that the woman's son, my boyfriend,
was responsible. I invented a scenario where he had
had a little heart-to-heart with his mother and had confessed that his only objection to me was that my breasts
were small; his mother then took it upon herself to
help out. Now I think I was wrong about the incident.
The mother was acting on her own, I think: that was
her way of being cruel and competitive under the guise
of being helpful and maternal. You have small breasts,
she was saying; therefore you will never make him as
happy as I have. Or you have small breasts; therefore
you will doubtless have sexual problems. Or you have
small breasts; therefore you are less woman than I am.
She was, as it happens, only the first of what seems to
me to be a never-ending string of women who have
made competitive remarks to me about breast size. "I
would love to wear a dress like that," my friend Emily
says to me, "but my bust is too big." Like that. Why do
women say these things to me? Do I attract these remarks the way other women attract married men or
alcoholics or homosexuals? This summer, for example.
I am at a party in East Hampton and I am introduced to
a woman from Washington. She is a minor celebrity,
very pretty and Southern and blond and outspoken,
and I am flattered because she has read something I
have written. We are talking animatedly, we have been
talking no more than five minutes, when a man comes
up to join us. "Look at the two of us," the woman says
to the man, indicating me and her. "The two of us together couldn't fill an A cup." Why does she say that? It
isn't even true, dammit, so why? Is she even more ad-

dled than I am on this subject? Does she honestly believe there is something wrong with her size breasts, which, it seems to me, now that I look hard at them, are just right? Do I unconsciously bring out competitiveness in women? In that form? What did I do to deserve it?

As for men.

There were men who minded and let me know that they minded. There were men who did not mind. In any case, *I* always minded.

And even now, now that I have been countlessly reassured that my figure is a good one, now that I am grown-up enough to understand that most of my feelings have very little to do with the reality of my shape, I am nonetheless obsessed by breasts. I cannot help it. I grew up in the terrible fifties—with rigid stereotypical sex roles, the insistence that men be men and dress like men and women be women and dress like women, the intolerance of androgyny—and I cannot shake it, cannot shake my feelings of inadequacy. Well, that time is gone, right? All those exaggerated examples of breast worship are gone, right? Those women were freaks, right? I know all that. And yet here I am, stuck with the psychological remains of it all, stuck with my own peculiar version of breast worship. You probably think I am crazy to go on like this: here I have set out to write a confession that is meant to hit you with the shock of recognition, and instead you are sitting there thinking I am thoroughly warped. Well, what can I tell you? If I had had them, I would have been a completely different person. I honestly believe that.

After I went into therapy, a process that made it possible for me to tell total strangers at cocktail parties that breasts were the hang-up of my life, I was often told that I was insane to have been bothered by my condition. I was also frequently told, by close friends, that I was extremely boring on the subject. And my girl friends, the ones with nice big breasts, would go on endlessly about how their lives had been far more miserable than mine. Their bra straps were snapped in class. They couldn't sleep on their stomachs. They were stared at whenever the word "mountain" cropped up in geography. And *Evangeline,* good God what they went through every time someone had to stand up and recite the Prologue to Longfellow's *Evangeline:* ". . . stand like druids of eld . . ./ With beards that rest on their bosoms." It was much worse for them, they tell me. They had a terrible time of it, they assure me. I don't know how lucky I was, they say.

I have thought about their remarks, tried to put myself in their place, considered their point of view. I think they are full of shit.

May, 1972

Fantasies

One of the trump cards that men who are threatened by women's liberation are always dredging up is the question of whether there is sex after liberation. I have heard at least five or six experts or writers or spokesmen or some such stand up at various meetings and wonder aloud what happens to sex between men and women when the revolution comes. These men are always hooted down by the women present; in fact, I am usually one of the women present hooting them down, sniggering snide remarks to whoever is next to me like well-we-certainly-know-how-sure-of-himself-*he*-is. This fall, at the *Playboy* Writers' Convocation, an author named Morton Hunt uttered the magic words at a panel on The Future of Sex, and even in that room, full of male chauvinism and *Playboy* philosophers, the animosity against him was audible.

I spend a great deal of my energy these days trying to fit feminism into marriage, or vice versa—I'm never sure which way the priorities lie; it depends on my mood—but as truly committed as I am to the movement and as violent as I have become toward people who knock it, I think it is unfair to dismiss these men. They deserve some kind of answer. Okay. The answer is, nobody knows what happens to sex after liberation. It's a big mystery. And now that I have gotten that out of the way, I can go on to what really interests and puzzles me about sex and liberation—which is that it is difficult for me to see how sexual behavior and relations between the sexes can change at all unless our sexual

12

fantasies change. So many of the conscious and unconscious ways men and women treat each other have to do with romantic and sexual fantasies that are deeply ingrained, not just in society but in literature. The movement may manage to clean up the mess in society, but I don't know whether it can ever clean up the mess in our minds.

I am somewhat liberated by current standards, but I have in my head this dreadful unliberated sex fantasy. One of the women in my consciousness-raising group is always referring to her "rich fantasy life," by which I suppose she means that in her fantasies she makes it in costume, or in exotic places, or with luminaries like Mao Tse-tung in a large bowl of warm Wheatena. My fantasy life is unfortunately nowhere near that interesting.

Several years ago, I went to interview photographer Philippe Halsman, whose notable achievements include a charming book containing photographs of celebrities jumping. The jumps are quite revealing in a predictable sort of way—Richard Nixon with his rigid, constricted jump, the Duke and Duchess of Windsor in a deeply dependent jump. And so forth. In the course of the interview, Halsman asked me if I wanted to jump for him; seeing it as a way to avoid possibly years of psychoanalysis, I agreed. I did what I thought was my quintessential jump. "Do it again," said Halsman. I did, attempting to duplicate exactly what I had done before. "Again," he said, and I did. "Well," said Halsman, "I can see from your jump that you are a very determined, ambitious, directed person, but you will never write a novel." "Why is that?" I asked. "Because you have only one jump in you," he said.

At the time, I thought that was really unfair—I had, after all, thought he wanted to see the *same* jump, not a different one every time; but I see now that he was exactly right. I have only one jump in me. I see this more and more every day. I am no longer interested in thirty-one flavors; I stick with English toffee. More to the point, I have had the same sex fantasy, with truly minor variations, since I was about eleven years old. It is really a little weird to be stuck with something so crucially important for so long; I have managed to rid myself of all the other accouterments of being eleven —I have pimples more or less under control, I can walk fairly capably in high heels—but I find myself with this appalling fantasy that has burrowed in and has absolutely nothing to do with my life.

I have never told anyone the exact details of my particular sex fantasy: it is my only secret and I am not going to divulge it here. I once told *almost* all of it to my former therapist; he died last year, and when I saw his obituary I felt a great sense of relief: the only person in the world who almost knew how crazy I am was gone and I was safe. Anyway, without giving away any of the juicy parts, I can tell you that in its broad outlines it has largely to do with being dominated by faceless males who rip my clothes off. That's just about all they have to do. Stare at me in this faceless way, go mad with desire, and rip my clothes off. It's terrific. In my sex fantasy, nobody ever loves me for my mind.

The fantasy of rape—of which mine is in a kind of prepubescent sub-category—is common enough among women and (in mirror image) among men. And what I don't understand is that with so many of us stuck with these clichéd feminine/masculine, submissive/dominant, masochistic/sadistic fantasies, how are we ever going to adjust fully to the less thrilling but more desirable reality of equality? A few months ago, someone named B. Lyman Steward, a urologist at Cedars of Lebanon Hospital in Los Angeles, attributed the rising frequency of impotence among his male patients to the women's movement, which he called an effort to dominate men. The movement is nothing of the kind; but it and a variety of other events in society have certainly brought about a change in the way women behave in bed. A young man who grows up expecting to dominate sexually is bound to be somewhat startled by a young woman who wants sex as much as he does, and multi-orgasmic sex at that. By the same token, I suspect that a great deal of the difficulty women report in achieving orgasm is traceable—sadly—to the possibility that a man who is a tender fellow with implicit capabilities for impotence hardly fits into classic fantasies of big brutes with implicit capabilities for violence. A close friend who has the worst marriage I know—her husband beats her up regularly—reports that her sex life is wonderful. I am hardly suggesting that women ask their men to beat them—nor am I advocating the course apparently preferred by one of the most prominent members of the women's movement, who makes it mainly with blue-collar workers and semiliterates. But I wonder how we will ever break free from all the nonsense we grew up with; I wonder if our fantasies can ever catch up to what we all want for our lives.

It is possible, through sheer willpower, to stop having unhealthy sex fantasies. I have several friends who did just that. "What do you have instead?" I asked. "Nothing," they replied. Well, I don't know. I'm not at all sure I wouldn't rather have an unhealthy sex fantasy than no sex fantasy at all. But my real question is whether it is possible, having discarded the fantasy, to discard the thinking and expectations it represents. In my case, I'm afraid it wouldn't be. I have no desire to be dominated. Honestly I don't. And yet I find myself becoming angry when I'm not. My husband has trouble hailing a cab or flagging a waiter, and suddenly I feel a kind of rage; ball-breaking anger rises to my T-zone. I wish he were better at hailing taxis than I am; on the other hand, I realize that expectation is culturally conditioned, utterly foolish, has nothing to do with anything, is exactly the kind of thinking that ought to be got rid of in our society; on still another hand, having that insight into my reaction does not seem to calm my irritation.

My husband is fond of reminding me of the story of Moses, who kept the Israelites in the desert for forty years because he knew a slave generation could not found a new free society. The comparison with the women's movement is extremely apt, I think; I doubt that it will ever be possible for the women of my generation to escape from our own particular slave mentality. For the next generation, life may indeed be freer. After all, if society changes, the fantasies will change; where women are truly equal, where their status has nothing to do with whom they marry, when the issues of masculine/feminine cease to exist, some of this absurd reliance on role playing will be eliminated. But not all of it. Because even after the revolution, we will be left with all the literature. "What will happen to the literature?" Helen Dudar of the New York *Post* once asked Ti-Grace Atkinson. "What does it matter what happens?" Ms. Atkinson replied. But it does. You are what you eat. After liberation, we will still have to reckon with the Sleeping Beauty and Cinderella. Granted there will also be a new batch of fairy tales about princesses who refuse to have ladies-in-waiting because it is exploitative of the lower classes—but that sounds awfully tedious, doesn't it? Short of a mass book burning, which no one wants, things may well go on as they are now: women pulled between the intellectual attraction of liberation and the emotional, psychological, and cultural mishmash it's hard to escape growing up with; men trying to cope with these two extremes, and with their own ambivalence besides. It's not much fun this way, but at least it's not boring.

July, 1972

On Never
Having Been
a Prom Queen

The other night, a friend of mine sat down at the table and informed me that if I was going to write a column about women, I ought to deal straight off with the subject most important to women in all the world. "What is that?" I asked. "Beauty," she said. I must have looked somewhat puzzled—as indeed I was—because she then went into a long and painful opening monologue about how she was losing her looks and I had no idea how terrible it was and that just recently an insensitive gentleman friend had said to her, "Michelle, you used to be such a beauty." I have no idea if this woman is really losing her looks—I have known her only a couple of years, and she looks pretty much the same to me—but she is certainly right in saying that I have no idea of what it is like. One of the few advantages to not being beautiful is that one usually gets better-looking as one gets older; I am, in fact, at this very moment gaining my looks. But what interested me about my response to my friend was that rather than feeling empathy for her—and I like to think I am fairly good at feeling empathy—I felt nothing. I like her very much, respect her, even believe she believes she is losing her looks, recognize her pain, but I just couldn't get into it.

Only a few days later, a book called *Memoirs of an*

Ex-Prom Queen, by Alix Kates Shulman (Knopf), arrived in the mail. Shulman, according to the jacket flap, had written a "bitterly funny" book about "being female in America." I would like to read such a book. I would like to write such a book. As it turns out, however, Alix Shulman hasn't. What she has written is a book about the anguish and difficulty of being beautiful. And I realized, midway through the novel, that if there is anything more boring to me than the problems of big-busted women, it is the problems of beautiful women.

"They say it's worse to be ugly," Shulman writes. "I think it must only be different. If you're pretty, you are subject to one set of assaults; if you're plain you are subject to another. Pretty, you may have more men to choose from, but you have more anxiety too, knowing your looks, which really have nothing to do with you, will disappear. Pretty girls have few friends. Kicked out of mankind in elementary school, and then kicked out of womankind in junior high, pretty girls have a lower birthrate and a higher mortality. It is the beauties like Marilyn Monroe who swallow twenty-five Nembutals on a Saturday night and kill themselves in their thirties."

Now I could take that paragraph one sentence at a time and pick nits (What about the pretty girls who *have* friends? What has Marilyn Monroe's death to do with all this? What does it mean to say that pretty girls have a lower birthrate—that they have fewer children or that there are less of them than there are of us?), but I prefer to say simply that it won't wash. There isn't an ugly girl in America who wouldn't exchange her problems for the problems of being beautiful; I don't believe there's a beautiful girl anywhere who would honestly prefer not to be. "They say it's worse to be ugly," Alix Shulman writes. Yes, they do say that. And they're right. It's also worse to be poor, worse to be orphaned, worse to be fat. Not just *different* from rich, familied, and thin—actually worse.

(I am a little puzzled as to why Ms. Shulman uses the words "plain" and "ugly" interchangeably; the difference between plain and ugly is as vast as the one between plain and pretty. As William Raspberry pointed out in a recent Washington *Post* column, ugly women are the most overlooked victims of discrimination in America.)

The point of all this is not about beauty—I hope I have made it clear that I don't know enough about beauty to make a point—but about divisions. I am separated from Alix Shulman and am in fact almost unable to judge her work because she is obsessed with being beautiful and I am obsessed with not being beautiful. We might as well be on separate sides altogether. And what makes me sad about the women's movement in general is my own inability, and that of so many other women, to get across such gulfs, to join hands, to unite on anything.

The women's liberation movement at this point in history makes the American Communist Party of the 1930s look like a monolith. I have been to meetings where the animosity between the gay and straight women was so strong and so unpleasant that I could not bear to be in the room. That is the most dramatic division in the movement, and one that has considerably slowed its forward momentum; but there are so many others. There is acrimony between the single and married women, working women and housewives, childless women and mothers. I have even heard a woman defend her affection for cooking to an incredulous group who believed that to cook at all—much less to like it—was to swallow the worst sort of cultural conditioning. Once I tried to explain to a fellow feminist why I liked wearing makeup; she replied by explaining why she does not. Neither of us understood a word the other said.

Every so often, I turn on the television and see one of the movement leaders being asked some idiot question like, "Isn't the women's movement in favor of all women abandoning their children and going off to work?" (I can hear David Susskind asking it now.) The leader usually replies that the movement isn't in favor of all women doing anything; what the movement is about, she says, is options. She is right, of course. At its best, that is exactly what the movement is about. But it just doesn't work out that way. Because the hardest thing for us to accept is the right to those options. I hear myself saying those words: *What this movement is about is options.* I say it to friends who are frustrated, or housebound, or guilty, or child-laden, and what I am really thinking is, If you really got it together, the option you would choose is mine.

I would like to be able to leap across the gulf that divides me from Alix Shulman. After all, her experience is not totally foreign to me: once I had a date with someone who thought I was beautiful. He talked all night, while I—who spent years developing my conversational ability to compensate for my looks (my life has been spent in compensation)—said nothing. At the end of the evening, he made a pass at me and I was insulted. So I understand. I recognize that people who are beautiful have problems. But so do people who get upset stomachs from raw onions, and men with blue-orange color blindness, and left-handed persons everywhere. I just can't get into it; what interests me these days tends to have more to do with the problems of women who were not prom queens in high school. I'm sorry about this—my point of view is not fair to Alix Shulman, or to my friend who thinks she is losing her looks, or to me, or to the movement. But that's where it is. I'm working on it. Like all things about liberation, sisterhood is difficult.

August, 1972

The Girls
in the Office

I have not looked at *The Best of Everything* since I first bought it—in paperback—ten years ago, but I have a perverse fondness for it. In case you somehow missed it, *The Best of Everything* was a novel by Rona Jaffe about the lives of four, or was it five, single women in New York; it was pretty good trash, as trash goes, which is not why I am fond of it. I liked it because it seemed to me that it caught perfectly the awful essence of being a single woman in a big city. False pregnancies. Real pregnancies. Abortions. Cads. Dark bars with married men. Rampant masochism. I remember particularly a sequence in the book where one of the girls, rejected by a lover, goes completely bonkers and begins spending all her time spying on him, poking through his garbage for discarded love letters and old potato peelings; ultimately, as I recall, she falls from his fire escape to her death. The story seemed to me only barely exaggerated from what I was seeing around me, and, I am sorry to say, doing myself.

I was, naturally, single when I read the novel, unhappily single, mired in the Dorothy Parker telephone-call syndrome ("Please, God, let him telephone me now. . . . I'll count five hundred by fives, and if he hasn't called me then, I will know God isn't going to help me, ever again. That will be the sign. Five, ten, fifteen . . .") and well aware of its hopeless

21

banality. It occurred to me as I read *The Best of Everything* that it would be practically impossible to write an accurate novel about the quality of life for single women in New York without writing a B novel, for the simple reason that life for single women in New York *is* a B novel. Even Dorothy Parker's short story about the phone call, horribly accurate—a classic, even—belongs in the pages of *Cosmopolitan* magazine.

I like to think that things have changed since my early years in New York. A lot has happened in the world, clearly. The women's movement, birth-control pills, legalized abortions in New York—life ought to have changed in some way. I want very much to believe this; like many married women, I have managed to romanticize my single years beyond recognition and I spend a lot of time daydreaming about what it would have been like to be single knowing then what I know now—or simply what it would be like to be single again.

In any event, I have just read a book that is enough to make me stop daydreaming for at least a week or two. Actually it's not a good book, or even a book in any real sense, but a series of tape-recorded interviews with fifteen single women who all work in the same New York office (Time-Life, thinly disguised). It is called *The Girls in the Office* (Simon & Schuster) and it has an incredibly old-fashioned, *Best of Everything*, trash epic quality: it is full of dreadful cartoon people who seem straight out of every junky fifties novel—the difference being, of course, that *The Girls in the Office* is nonfiction, real, an honest-to-God case of life imitating trash. Its author, Jack Olsen, has not really written anything; he has instead been content merely to edit the tapes, neaten up the interviews, give them snappy endings, reconstruct them to the point where they seem too pat, too slick, too much, maybe not even true. But they are true, I'm afraid. Bizarre and weird, but true. And because they are, the book, in its sleazy, slapdash, pseudo-sociological way, is fascinating—both for what it says about the women as for the men in their lives.

The women in *The Girls in the Office* range from twenty-four to fifty years old and all of them live alone in Manhattan, surrounded and—as they testify—tormented by exhibitionists, flashers, rapists, muggers, goosers, breathers, feelers, and Peeping Toms. Almost none of them has an executive-level job, and none seems to have ambitions toward anything higher. Their competitiveness is directed solely toward other women; their energies are spent scrambling for little favors and petty advances within the lower realm of the company reserved for women only. That men are responsible for keeping them down does not seem to have occurred to them; in any case, they are not interested in getting up from under. What they are looking for is a husband. In the meantime, they want not a better slot but a comfortable niche, the warm feeling of working in a nice, big, air-conditioned, wall-to-wall carpeted office full of friendly faces and office parties. The office becomes their world, the employees their surrogate family. As one of the women explains: "[We're] producing a product in close conjunction with brilliant men, just as married couples produce children." The men—most of them married—dominate it all, flirt with them, date them, seduce them, string them along, and manage to convince them that all of it is worth it to spend time with such extraordinary creatures. "You have to learn quickly that the super-talented, super-creative geniuses in our company are different from other men," says one of the women in the book. Says another: "The hotshots at The Company [are] so glamorous. How could I get interested in a fifth assistant teller at a bank in the Bronx, when the man in the next cubicle at the office has just got back from Hong Kong?"

The parade of married men who traipse through these women's apartments turns their lives into parodies of *Back Street*. The women wait, year after year, for the men to leave their wives. They never do. Year after year of one or two nights a week, furtive lunches, nooners at midtown hotels, tacky confrontations with their wives. Even the girls who manage to avoid the married men make a mess of their lives. A few become tough in a way that is simply inhumane: "I learned how to turn the men's lust against them. I'd pretend to be interested in one of them and I'd get him to talk to me for three hours and let him think he was making a great successful pass, and then I'd turn around and leave!" The rest manage to come up with relationships with single men that are quite as demeaning and unhealthy as those with married men. One woman Olsen calls Jayne Gouldtharpe has an affair for a year with an insurance man whose idea of rebellion is to throw egg yolks at the wall. After a year or so of what Nichols and May used to call proximity but no relating, he comes over for dinner one night. "We were taking a shower together," Jayne recalls, "and he said, 'You know, all we ever talk about is you. I have problems too. . . .'

" 'What do you mean?'

" 'Well, I'm going to Italy tomorrow for a long visit, and my big problem is how to tell you that this is the last time we'll ever be together.' "

After two days of misery, Jayne takes a week off from work, flies to Rome with no idea of where her lover is staying, and spends seven days looking for him. She returns to New York, only to find that he had never intended to go to Italy in the first place. "He was a sadist dealing with a masochist," she concludes, "and the ultimate bit of sadism was to stand in my shower naked and tell me that we were through."

There is another woman in the book Olsen calls Gloria Rolstin, who falls in love with an executive named Tom Lantini. (Names are not Olsen's strong point.) Lantini is divorced and lives with his invalid mother in a town house downtown. Within a few months, he has moved Gloria in as an ersatz nurse's aide: she changes his mother's clothes, takes her to the bathroom, cleans up after her, feeds her medicine, plays honeymoon bridge—"And the old lady barely able to tell what was trump!" All the while, she sleeps alone on a couch downstairs while Tom and his mother sleep in adjoining bedrooms above.

The affair between Gloria and Tom, such as it is, lasts seven years, the last three or four punctuated by a long series of physical brawls—"He cut my nose. I sprained his wrist. He blackened my eye. I pulled out about five square inches of his curls. . . . He smashed me so hard on the side of my head that he knocked me down, and my ear was ripped open from his ring. . . ." And so forth. The acts of violence become so commonplace in this book that at one point, when one Vanessa Van Durant is locked in her apartment by her boyfriend and beaten and buggered for two weeks, I found myself shrugging and thinking, Ah, yes, the old lock-her-in-the-apartment-and-beat-her-and-bugger-her routine. What is most frightening about all these fights is not just their frequency but that the women accept it as a matter of course, and even blame themselves for it. "I'll get a little pushy or a little whiny," one explains, "and a man will haul off and smack me. It's usually my own fault." I'm a masochist, he's a sadist; I drove him to it; it's as simple as that. It is, of course, nowhere near as simple as that. I don't pretend to be able to provide an answer as to why these women put up with what they do, but some of it has to do with a society structured in such a way as to make women believe that to be with a man— any man, on whatever terms—is better than being alone. Only one of the women sees the women's movement as providing any relevance to her situation. The rest want nothing to do with it. Says one: "I endorse the economic side of Women's Lib completely, but I don't go around marching or burning my bra, because I think things like that only tend to emasculate men, and the New York male has already been emasculated beyond recognition."

The men in this book are in every way as pathetic as the women they victimize. I could give example after example. There is a chronically impotent married man who attempts to seduce several of the women in this book and always insists the problem has merely to do with too much liquor. ("Foreplay is fine for about an hour," says one of the women who becomes involved with him, "but when it goes on for a month, that's a pretty good sign something's very wrong.") There is an executive, Peter-principled into a job he cannot handle, who hangs on and spends his time whacking off while dictating letters to his secretary. There is another man who becomes so disturbed when his girl breaks off their affair that he sends her a hot-pepper explosive in the mail, telephones her all night and hangs up, substitutes Drano for salt in her salt shakers, and slips a vial of acid into her loafers which burns her toes.

One of the themes the women return to frequently in *The Girls in the Office* is their belief that men are just little boys, infants with "hang-ups in their brains like spider webs." I have heard this theme song so many times from so many women; and every time I hear it, I recoil. It is, quite obviously, a profoundly anti-male remark; it is also, I'm afraid, partly true. Saying it's so gets us nowhere, though. The unhappy corollary to the fact that a lot of men are just little boys is the fact that so many women put up with it —cater to it, in fact, mother them, bolster their egos by subjugating their own—and feed right into the real problem, which is not that men are little boys but that men don't like women very much, can't deal with their demands, their sexuality, their equality. The role of a corporation like Time-Life in this—which underlines the pattern by delivering to each male employee a secretary or researcher he can dominate—would make an interesting book. The lives of fifteen single women in New York would also make an interesting book someday. This one isn't it.

September, 1972

Reunion

A boy and a girl are taking a shower together in the bathroom. How to explain the significance of it? It is a Friday night in June, the first night of the tenth reunion of the Class of 1962 of Wellesley College, and a member of my class has just returned from the bathroom with the news. A boy and a girl are taking a shower together. No one can believe it. Ten years and look at the changes. Ten years ago, we were allowed men in the rooms on Sunday afternoons only, on the condition the door be left fourteen inches ajar. One Sunday during my freshman year, a girl in my dormitory went into her room with a date and not only closed the door but put a sock on it. (The sock—I feel silly remembering nonsense like this, but I do—was a Wellesley signal meaning "Do Not Disturb.") Three hours later, she and the boy emerged and she was wearing a different outfit. No one could believe it. We were that young. Today boys on exchange programs from MIT and Dartmouth live alongside the girls, the dormitory doors lock, and some of the women in my class—as you can see from the following excerpt from one letter to our tenth-reunion record book—have been through some changes themselves:

"In the past five years I have (1) had two children and two abortions, (2) moved seriously into politics, working up to more responsible positions on bigger campaigns, (3) surrendered myself to what I finally acknowledged was my lifework—the women's revolution, (4) left my husband and children to seek my

28

fortune and on the way (5) fallen desperately, madly, totally in love with a beautiful man and am sharing a life with him in Cambridge near Harvard Square where we're completely incredibly happy doing the work we love and having amazing life adventures."

I went back to my reunion at Wellesley to write about it. I'm doing a column, that's why I'm going, I said to New York friends who were amazed that I would want anything to do with such an event. I want to see what happened, I said—to my class, to the college. (I didn't say that I wanted my class and the college to see what had happened to me, but that of course was part of it, too.) A few years ago, Wellesley went through a long reappraisal before rejecting coeducation and reaffirming its commitment to educating women; that interested me. Also, I wondered how my class, almost half of which has two or more children, was dealing with what was happening to women today. On Friday evening, when my classmate and I arrived at the dormitory that was our class headquarters, we bumped into two Wellesley juniors. One of them asked straight off if we wanted to see their women's liberation bulletin board. They took us down the corridor to a cork board full of clippings, told us of their battle to have a full-time gynecologist on campus, and suddenly it became important for us to let them know we were not what they thought. We were not those alumnae who came back to Wellesley because it was the best time of their lives; we were not those cardigan-sweatered, Lilly Pulitzered matrons or Junior League members or League of Women Voters volunteers; we were not about to be baited by their bulletin board. We're not Them. I didn't come to reunion because I wanted to. I'm here to write about it. Understand?

Wellesley College has probably the most beautiful campus in the country, more lush and gorgeous than any place I have ever seen. In June, the dogwood and azalea are in bloom around Lake Waban, the ivy spurts new growth onto the collegiate Gothic buildings, the huge maples are obscenely loaded with shade. So idyllic, in the literal sense—an idyll before a rude awakening. There was Wellesley, we were told, and then, later, there would be the real world. The real world was different. "Where, oh where are the staid alumnae?" goes a song Wellesley girls sing, and they answer, "They've gone out from their dreams and theories. Lost, lost in the wide, wide world." At Wellesley we would be allowed to dream and theorize. We would be taken seriously. It would not always be so.

Probably the most insidious influence on the students ten years ago was the one exerted by the class deans. They were a group of elderly spinsters who believed that the only valuable role for Wellesley graduates was to go on to the only life the deans knew anything about —graduate school, scholarship, teaching. There was no value at all placed on achievement in the so-called real world. Success of that sort was suspect; worse than that, it was unserious. Better to be a housewife, my dear, and to take one's place in the community. *Keep a hand in.* This policy was not just implicit but was actually articulated. During my junior year, in a romantic episode that still embarrasses me, I became engaged to a humorless young man whose primary attraction was that he was fourth in his class at Harvard Law School. I went to see my class dean about transferring to Barnard senior year before being married. "Let me give you some advice," she told me. "You have worked so hard at Wellesley. When you marry, take a year off. Devote yourself to your husband and your marriage." I was incredulous. To begin with, I had not worked hard at Wellesley—anyone with my transcript in front of her ought to have been able to see that. But far more important, I had always intended to work after college; my mother was a career woman who had successfully indoctrinated me and my sisters that to be a housewife was to be nothing. Take a year off being a wife? Doing what? I carried the incident around with me for years, repeating it from time to time as positive proof that Wellesley wanted its graduates to be merely housewives. Then, one day, I met a woman who had graduated ten years before me. She had never wanted anything but to be married and have children; she, too, had gone to see this dean before leaving Wellesley and marrying. "Let me give you some advice," the dean told her. "Don't have children right away. Take a year to work." And so I saw. What Wellesley wanted was for us to avoid the extremes, to be instead that thing in the middle. Neither a rabid careerist nor a frantic mamma. That thing in the middle: a trustee. "Life is not all dirty diapers and runny noses," writes Susan Connard Chenoweth in the class record. "I do make it into the real world every week to present a puppet show on ecology called *Give a Hoot, Don't Pollute.*" The deans would be proud of Susan. She is on her way. A doer of good works. An example to the community. Above all, a Samaritan.

I never went near the Wellesley College chapel in my four years there, but I am still amazed at the amount of Christian charity that school stuck us all with, a kind of glazed politeness in the face of boredom and stupidity. Tolerance, in the worst sense of the word. Wellesley was not alone in encouraging this for its students, but it always seemed so sad that a school that could have done so much for women put so much energy into the one area women should be educated out of. How marvelous it would have been to go to a women's college that encouraged impoliteness, that rewarded aggression, that encouraged argument. Women by the time they are eighteen are so damaged, so beaten down, so tyrannized out of behaving in all the wonderful outspoken ways unfortunately characterized as masculine; a college committed to them has to take on the burden of repair—of remedial education, really. I'm not just talking about vocational guidance and placement bureaus (which are

far more important than anyone at these schools believes) but also about the need to force young women
to define themselves before they abdicate the task and
become defined by their husbands. *What do you think?
What is your opinion?* No one ever asked. We all
graduated from Wellesley able to describe everything
we had studied—Baroque painting, Hindemith, Jack-
sonian democracy, Yeats—yet we were never asked
what we thought of any of it. *Do you like it? Do you
think it is good? Do you know that even if it is good
you do not have to like it?* During reunion weekend,
at the Saturday-night class supper, we were subjected
to an hour of dance by a fourth-rate Boston theatre
ensemble which specializes in eighth-rate Grotowski
crossed with the worst of *Marat/Sade.* Grunts. Moans.
Jumping about imitating lambs. It was absolutely awful. The next day, a classmate with the improbable
name of Muffy Kleinfeld asked me what I thought of
it. "What did *you* think of it?" I replied. "Well," she
said, "I thought their movements were quite expressive
and forceful, but I'm not exactly sure what they were
trying to do dramatically." *But what did you think of
it?*

I am probably babbling a bit here, but I feel a real
anger toward Wellesley for blowing it, for being so
damned irrelevant. Like many women involved with
the movement, I have come full circle in recent years:
I used to think that anything exclusively for women
(women's pages, women's colleges, women's novels)
was a bad idea. Now I am all in favor of it. But when
Wellesley decided to remain a women's college, it
seemed so pointless to me. Why remain a school for
women unless you are prepared to deal with the
problems women have in today's society? Why bother?
If you are simply going to run a classy liberal-arts
college in New England, an ivory tower for $3,900 a
year, why not let the men in?

Wellesley *has* changed. Some of the changes are
superficial: sex in the dorms, juicy as it is, probably
has more to do with the fact that it is 1972 than

with real change. On the other hand, there are changes that are almost fundamental. The spinster deans are mostly gone. There is a new president, and she has actually been married. Twice. Many of the hangovers from an earlier era—when Wellesley was totally a school for the rich as opposed to now, when it is only partially so—have been eliminated: sit-down dinners with maids and students waiting on tables; Tree Day, a spring rite complete with tree maidens and tree plantings; the freshman-class banner hunt. Hoop rolling goes on, but this year a feminist senior won and promptly denounced the rite as trivial and sexist. Bible is no longer required. More seniors are applying to law school. "They are not as polite as you were," says history professor Edward Gulick, which sounds promising. Yet another teacher tells me that the students today are more like us than like the class of 1970. The graduation procession is an endless troupe of look-alikes, cookie-cutter perfect faces with long straight hair parted in the middle. Still, there are at least three times as many black faces among them as there were in my time.

And there is the graduation speaker, Eleanor Holmes Norton, a black who is New York City Commissioner of Human Rights. Ten years ago, our speaker was Santha Rama Rau, who bored us mightily with a low-keyed speech on the need to put friendship above love of country. The contrast is quite extraordinary: Norton, an outspoken feminist and mesmerizing public speaker, raises her fist to the class as she speaks. "The question has been asked," she says, " 'What is a woman? A woman is a person who makes choices. A woman is a dreamer. A woman is a planner. A woman is a maker, and a molder. A woman is a person who makes choices. A woman builds bridges. A woman makes children and makes cars. A woman writes poetry and songs. A woman is a person who makes choices. You cannot even simply become a mother anymore. You must *choose* motherhood. Will you choose change? Can you become its vanguard?" It is a moving speech, full of comparisons between women today and the young blacks of the 1960s; midway through, a Madras-jacketed father, absolutely furious, storms down the aisle, collars his graduating daughter, and drags her off to tell her what he thinks of it. She returns a few minutes later to join her class in a standing ovation.

As for my class, two things are immediately apparent. The housewives, who are openly elated at being sprung from the responsibility of children for a weekend, are nonetheless very defensive about women's liberation and wary of those of us who have made other choices. In the class record book, the most common expression is "women's lib notwithstanding," as in this from Janet Barton Mostafa: "I'm thrilled to find, women's lib to the contrary notwithstanding, that mother-hood is a pretty joyful experience. Shakespeare will have to wait in the wings a year or two." *You cannot even simply become a mother anymore. You must choose motherhood.* "I steeled myself against coming," one of the housewives said at reunion. "I was sure I was going to have to defend myself." Neither she nor any other housewife will have to defend herself this trip; we are all far too polite. Still, it is interesting that the housewives—not the working mothers or the single or divorced women—are self-conscious. Which brings me to the second trend: the number of women at reunion who are not just divorced but proudly divorced, wearing their new independence as a kind of badge. I cannot imagine that previous Wellesley reunions attracted any divorced women at all.

On Saturday afternoon, our class meets formally. The meeting is conducted by the outgoing class president, B. J. Diener, the developer of Breck One Dandruff Shampoo. She has brought each of us a bottle of the stuff, a gesture some of the class think is in poor taste. I think it is sweet. B J. is saying that the college ought to do more for its alumnae—hold symposia around the country, provide reading lists on selected subjects, run correspondence courses for grad-uate-school credits. I find myself involved in a debate about the wisdom of all this—I hadn't meant to get involved, but here I am, with my hand up, about to say that it sounds suspiciously like suburban clubwomen. As it happens, I am sitting in the back with a small group of fellow troublemakers, and we all end up waving our hands and speaking out. "It seems to me," says one, "that all this is in the same spirit of elitism we've tried to get away from since leaving Wellesley." Says another: "Where is the leadership of Wellesley when it comes to graduate-school quotas for women? If Wellesley is going to stand out and be a special place for women, it should be standing up and making a loud noise about it." One thing leads to another, and the Class of 1962 ends up passing a unanimous resolution urging the college to take a position of leadership in the women's movement. It seems a stunning and miraculous victory, and so, giddy, we push on to yet another controversial topic. That morning, graduation exercises had been leafleted by a campus group urging Wellesley to sell its stocks in companies manufacturing products for war; we think the class should support them. President Diener thinks this is a terrible idea, and she musters all her Harvard Business School expertise to suggest instead that we ask the college to vote its shares against company management. Hands are up all over the room. "The whole purpose of Wellesley's investment is to make money," says one woman, "and I for one don't care if they want to invest it in whorehouses." The motion to urge the college to sell its war stocks is defeated 30–8. The eight of us leave together, flushed with the partial success of our troublemaking, and suddenly I feel depressed and silly. We had come back to make a little trouble but, like the senior who won hoop rolling and denounced it, we all tend toward tiny little rebellions, harmless nips at the system. We will never make any real trouble. Wellesley helped see to that.

And the nonsense. My God, the nonsense. At reunion, most of the students are gone and classes are over for the year. All that remains is a huge pile of tradition. Singing on the chapel steps. Fruit punch and tea in the afternoon. Class cheers and class songs. On Sunday morning, the last day of a hopelessly over-scheduled weekend, the reunion classes parade down to the alumnae meeting. Each class carries a felt banner and each woman wears a white dress decorated with some kind of costume insignia, also in class colors. My class is holding plastic umbrellas trimmed with huge bouquets of plastic violets and purple ribbons. The Class of 1957 is waving green feather dusters. Nineteen thirty-two is wearing what look like strawberry shortcakes but turn out to be huge red crowns; 1937 is in chefs' hats and aprons with signs reading, " '37 is alive and cooking!" I am standing on the side, defiant in my non-umbrellaness, as the Class of 1952 comes down the path with red backpacks strapped on; in the midst of them I see a woman I know, a book editor, who is marching with her class but is not wearing a backpack. I start to laugh, because it seems clear to me that we both think we are somehow set apart from all this—she because she is not wearing anything on her back, I because I am taking notes. We are both wrong, of course.

I can pretend that I have come back to Wellesley only because I want to write about it, but I am really here because I still care, I still care about this Mickey Mouse institution; I am foolish enough to think that someday it will do something important for women. That I care at all, that I am here at all, makes me one of Them. I am not exactly like them—I may be a better class of dumb—but we are all dumb. This college is about as meaningful to the educational process in America as a perfume factory is to the national economy. And all of us care, which makes us all idiots for wasting a minute thinking about the place.

October, 1972

Miami

It's about this mother-of-us-all business.

It is Sunday morning in Miami Beach, the day before the Democratic Convention is to begin, and the National Women's Political Caucus is holding a press conference. The cameras are clicking at Gloria, and Bella has swept in trailed by a vortex of television crews, and there is Betty, off to the side, just slightly out of frame. The cameras will occasionally catch a shoulder of her flowered granny dress or a stray wisp of her chaotic graying hair or one of her hands churning up the air; but it will be accidental, background in a photograph of Gloria, or a photograph of Bella, or a photograph of Gloria and Bella. Betty's eyes are darting back and forth trying to catch someone's attention, anyone's attention. No use, Gloria is speaking, and then Bella, and then Sissy Farenthold from Texas. And finally . . . Betty's lips tighten as she hears the inevitable introduction coming: "Betty Friedan, the mother of us all." That does it. "I'm getting sick and tired of this mother-of-us-all thing," she says. She is absolutely right, of course: in the women's movement, to be called the mother of anything is rarely a compliment. And what it means in this context, make no mistake, is that Betty, having in fact given birth, ought to cut the cord. Bug off. Shut up. At the very least, retire gracefully to the role of senior citizen, professor emeritus. Betty Friedan has no intention of doing anything of the kind. It's her baby, damn it. Her movement. Is she supposed to sit still and let a beautiful thin lady run off with it?

The National Women's Political Caucus (N.W.P.C.) was organized in July, 1971, by a shaky coalition of women's movement leaders. Its purpose was to help women in and into political life, particularly above the envelope-licking level. Just how well the caucus will do in its first national election remains to be seen, but in terms of the Democratic Convention it was wildly successful—so much so, in fact, that by the time the convention was to begin, the N.W.P.C. leaders were undergoing a profound sense of anticlimax. There were 1,121 women delegates, up from 13 percent four years ago to nearly 40 percent. There was a comprehensive and stunning women's plank in the platform; four years ago there was none. There were battles still to be fought at the convention—the South Carolina challenge and the abortion plank—but the first was small potatoes (or so it seemed beforehand) and the second was a guaranteed loser. And so, in a sense, the major function for the N.W.P.C. was to be ornamental —that is, it was simply to be *there*. Making its presence felt. Putting forth the best possible face. Pretending to a unity that did not exist. Above all, putting on a good show: the abortion plank would never carry, a woman would not be nominated as Vice-President this year, but the N.W.P.C. would put on a good show. Nineteen seventy-six, and all that. Punctuating all this would be what at times seemed an absurd emphasis on semantics: committees were run by "spokespersons" and "chairpersons"; phones were never manned but "womanned" and "personned." All this was public relations, not politics. They are two different approaches: the first is genteel, dignified, orderly, goes by the rules, and that was the one the women planned to play. They got an inadvertent baptism in the second primarily because George McGovern crossed them, but also because politics, after all, is the name of the game.

In 1963, Betty Friedan wrote *The Feminine Mystique* and became a national celebrity. She moved from the suburbs to Manhattan, separated from her husband, and began to devote much of her time to public speaking. She was a founder of the N.W.P.C. and of the National Organization for Women (N.O.W.), from whose national board she resigned voluntarily last year. This year she ran and lost as a Chisholm delegate to the convention. Among the high points of her campaign was a press release announcing she would appear in Harlem with a "Traveling Watermelon Feast" to distribute to the natives. In recent months, her influence within the movement has waned to the point that even when she is right (which she is occasionally, though usually for the wrong reasons), no one pays any attention to her. Two weeks before the convention, the N.W.P.C. council met to elect a spokesperson in Miami and chose Gloria Steinem over Friedan. The election was yet another chapter in Friedan's ongoing feud with Steinem—the two barely speak—and by the time Betty arrived in Miami she was furious. "I'm so disgusted with Gloria," she would mutter on her way to an N.W.P.C. meeting. Gloria was selling out the women. Gloria was ripping off the movement. Gloria was a tool of George McGovern. Gloria and Bella were bossing the delegates around. Gloria was part of a racist clique that would not support Shirley Chisholm for Vice-President. And so it went. Every day, Friedan would call N.W.P.C. headquarters at the dingy Betsy Ross Hotel downtown and threaten to call a press conference to expose the caucus; every day, at the meetings the N.W.P.C. held for press and female delegates, movement leaders would watch with a kind of horrified fascination to see what Betty Friedan would do next.

And Gloria. *Sic transit,* etc. Gloria Steinem has in the past year undergone a total metamorphosis, one that makes her critics extremely uncomfortable. Like Jane Fonda, she has become dedicated in a way that is a little frightening and almost awe-inspiring; she is demanding to be taken seriously—and it is the one demand her detractors, who prefer to lump her in with all the other radical-chic beautiful people, cannot bear to grant her. Once the glamour girl, all legs and short skirts and long painted nails, David Webb rings, Pucci, Gucci, you-name-it-she-had-it, once a fixture in gossip columns which linked her to one attractive man after another, she has managed to transform herself almost totally. She now wears Levi's and simple T-shirts—and often the same outfit two days running. The nails are as long as ever, but they are unpolished, and her fingers bare. She has managed to keep whatever private life she still has out of the papers. Most important, she projects a calm, peaceful, subdued quality; her humor is gentle, understated. Every so often, someone suggests that Gloria Steinem is only into the women's movement because it is currently the chic place to be; it always makes me smile, because she is about the only remotely chic thing connected with the movement.

It is probably too easy to go on about the two of them this way: Betty as Wicked Witch of the West, Gloria as Ozma, Glinda, Dorothy—take your pick. To talk this way ignores the subtleties, right? Gloria is not, after all, uninterested in power. And yes, she manages to remain above the feud, but that is partly because, unlike Betty, she has friends who will fight dirty for her. Still, it is hard to come out anywhere but squarely on her side. Betty Friedan in her thoroughly irrational hatred of Steinem, has ceased caring whether or not the effects of that hatred are good or bad for the women's movement. Her attack on Steinem in the August *McCall's,* which followed the convention by barely a week, quoted Steinem out of context

(Steinem's remark, "Marriage is prostitution," was made in the course of a speech on the effects of discrimination in marriage laws) and implied that Gloria was defiantly anti-male, a charge that is, of course, preposterous. I am not criticizing Friedan for discussing the divisions in the movement; nor do I object to her concern about man-haters; if she wants to air all that, it's okay with me. What I do not understand is why—for any but personal reasons—she chooses to discredit Steinem (and Bella Abzug) by tying them in with philosophies they have absolutely nothing to do with.

At a certain point in the convention, every N.W.P.C. meeting began to look and sound the same. Airless, windowless rooms decked with taffeta valances and Miami Beach plaster statuary. Gloria in her jeans and aviator glasses, quoting a female delegate on the gains women have made in political life this year: "It's like pushing marbles through a sieve. It means the sieve will never be the same again." Bella Abzug in her straw hat, bifocals cocked down on her nose, explaining that abortion is too a Constitutional right and belongs in a national platform. "I would like an attorney to advise us on this," says a New York delegate who believes it is a local matter. "One just did," Bella replies. Clancy and Sullivan, two women delegates from Illinois whose credentials are being challenged by the Daley machine, stand and are cheered. Germaine Greer, in overalls, takes notes quietly into a tiny tape recorder. Betty looks unhappy. The South Carolina challenge is discussed: the women want to add seven more delegates to the nine women already serving on the thirty-two member delegation. "Are these new delegates going to be women or wives?" asks one woman. "Because I'm from Missouri and we filed a challenge and now we have twelve new delegates who turned out to be sisters of wives, daughters of. . . . What is the point of having a woman on a delega-

tion who will simply say, 'Honey, how do we vote?' "
The microphone breaks down. "Until women control
technology," says Gloria, "we will have to be dependent in a situation like this." The days pass, and "Make
Policy Not Coffee" buttons are replaced by "Boycott
Lettuce" buttons are replaced by "Sissy for Vice-President" buttons. The days pass, and Betty is still somewhat under control.

The task Friedan ultimately busied herself with was
a drive to make Shirley Chisholm Vice-President, something Shirley Chisholm had no interest whatsoever in
becoming. Friedan began lobbying for this the Friday
before the convention began, when she asked the
N.W.P.C. to endorse Chisholm for Vice-President; the
council decided to hold back from endorsing anyone
until it was clear who wanted to run. And meanwhile it
would be ready with other women's names; among those
that came up were Farenthold, Abzug, Steinem, and
Representative Martha Griffiths. Jane Galvin Lewis, a
black who was representing Dorothy Height of the
National Council of Negro Women at the convention,
had suggested Steinem at the meeting. The night Shirley
Chisholm was to arrive in Miami, Lewis went up to the
Deauville Hotel to welcome her and bumped into Betty
Friedan in the lobby.

"What are you doing here?" Friedan asked.

"I'm here to meet Shirley," said Lewis.

"You really play both ends, don't you?" said Friedan.

"Explain that," said Lewis.

"What kind of black are you anyway?"

"What are you talking about?"

"You didn't even want to support Shirley Chisholm,"
Friedan said, her voice rising. "I heard you. I heard
you put up somebody else's name."

"That was after we decided to have a list ready,"
said Lewis. "Stop screaming at me."

"I'm going to do an exposé," shouted Friedan. "I'm
going to expose everyone. If it's the last thing I do,

I'm going to do it. I'm going to do it." She turned, walked off to a group of women, and left Jane Lewis standing alone.

"It's like pushing marbles through a sieve," Gloria is saying. Monday, opening day, and the N.W.P.C. is holding a caucus for women delegates to hear the Presidential candidates. Betty has publicly announced her drive to run Chisholm for Vice-President. The ballroom of the Carillon Hotel, packed full of boisterous, exuberant delegates, activists, and press, gives her suggestion a standing ovation; minutes later, it is hissing Chisholm with equal gusto for waffling on the California challenge. I am sitting next to Shirley MacLaine, McGovern's chief adviser on women's issues, and she is explaining to fellow delegate Marlo Thomas that McGovern will abandon the South Carolina challenge if there is any danger of its bringing up the procedural question of what constitutes a majority. McGovern, she is saying, plans to soft-pedal the challenge in his speech here—and here he is now, pushing through another standing ovation, beaming while he is graciously introduced by Liz Carpenter. "We know we wouldn't have been here if it hadn't been for you," she says. "George McGovern didn't talk about reform —he did something about it." The audience is McGovern's. "I am grateful for the introduction that all of you are here because of me," says the candidate rumored to be most in touch with women's issues. "But I really think the credit for that has to go to Adam instead. . . ." He pauses for the laugh and looks genuinely astonished when what he gets instead is a resounding hiss. "Can I recover if I say Adam and Eve?" he asks. Then he goes on to discuss the challenges, beginning with South Carolina. "On that challenge," he says, "you have my full and unequivocal support." Twelve hours later, the women find out that full and unequivocal support from George McGovern is considerably less than that.

"We were screwed," Debbie Leff is saying. Leff is press liaison for the N.W.P.C., and she is putting mildly what the McGovern forces did to the women. Monday night, the caucus, under floor leader Bella Abzug, delivered over 200 non-McGovern delegate votes on South Carolina—100 more than they had been told were necessary—and then watched, incredulous, as the McGovern staff panicked and pulled back its support. Tuesday night, the fight over the abortion plank—which was referred to as the "human-reproduction plank" because it never once mentioned the word "abortion"—produced the most emotional floor fight of the convention. The McGovern people had been opposed to the plank because they thought it would hurt his candidacy; at the last minute, they produced a right-to-lifer to give a seconding speech, a move they had promised the women they would not make. "Because of that pledge," said Steinem, "we didn't mention butchering women on kitchen tables in our speeches, and then they have a speaker who's saying, 'Next thing you know, they'll be murdering old people.'" Female members of the press lobbied for the plank. Male delegates left their seats to allow women alternates to vote. The movement split over whether to have a roll call or simply a voice vote. At four in the morning, Bella Abzug was screaming at Shirley MacLaine, and Steinem, in tears, was confronting McGovern campaign manager Gary Hart: "You promised us you would not take the low road, you bastards." The roll call on the plank was held largely at Betty Friedan's insistence. She and Martha McKay of North Carolina were the only N.W.P.C. leaders who were willing to take the risk; the rest thought the roll call would be so badly defeated that it would be best to avoid the humiliation. Friedan was in this case right for the wrong reasons: "We have to find out who our enemies are," she said. Incredibly, the plank went down to a thoroughly respectable defeat, 1572.80 against, 1101.37 for.

Thursday. A rumor is circulating that Gloria Steinem is at the Doral Hotel to speak with McGovern. I find her in the lobby. "I didn't see him," she says. "I don't want to see him." She is walking over to the Fontainebleau for a meeting; and on the way out of the Doral, Bob Anson, a former *Time* reporter, who interviewed her for a McGovern profile, says hello.

"At some point I'd like to talk to you about the socks," Gloria says.

"What do you mean?" asks Anson.

"You said in that article that I give him advice about socks and shirts. I don't talk to him about things like that. He listens to men about clothes."

Anson apologizes, claims he had nothing to do with the error, and as we leave the hotel, I suggest to Gloria that such incorrect facts stem from a kind of news-magazine tidbit madness.

"That's not it," says Gloria. "It's just that if you're a woman, all they can think about your relationship with a politician is that you're either sleeping with him or advising him about clothes." We start walking up Collins Avenue, past lettuce-boycott petitioners and welfare-rights pamphleteers. "It's just so difficult," she says, crying now. I begin babbling—all the pressures on you, no private life, no sleep, no wonder you're upset. "It's not that," says Gloria. "It's just that they won't take us seriously." She wipes at her cheeks with her hands, and begins crying again. "And I'm just tired of being screwed, and being screwed by my friends. By George McGovern, whom I raised half the money for in his first campaign, wrote his speeches. I can see him. I can get in to see him. That's easy. But what would be the point? He just doesn't understand. We went to see him at one point about abortion, and the question of welfare came up. 'Why are you concerned about welfare?' he said. He didn't understand it was a women's issue." She paused. "They won't take us seriously. We're just walking wombs. And the television coverage. Teddy White and Eric Sevareid saying that now that the women are here, next thing there'll be a caucus of left-handed Lithuanians." She is still crying, and I try to offer some reassuring words, something, but everything I say is wrong; I have never cried over anything remotely political in my life, and I honestly have no idea of what to say.

And so Friday, at last, and it is over. Sissy Farenthold has made a triumphant, albeit symbolic, run for the Vice-Presidency and come in second; as a final irony, she was endorsed by Shirley Chisholm. Jean Westwood is the new chairperson of the Democratic National Committee, although she prefers to be called chairman. I am talking to Martha McKay. "I'm fifty-two years old," she is saying. "I've gotten to the point where I choose what I spend time on. Look at the situation in North Carolina. Forty-four percent of the black women who work are domestics. In the eastern part of the state, some are making fifteen dollars a week and totin'. You know what that is? That's taking home roast beef, and that's supposed to make up for the wages. We're talking about bread on the table. We're talking about women who are heads of households who can't get credit. They hook up with a man, he signs the credit agreement, they make the payments, and in the end he owns the house. When things like this are going on in the country, who's got time to get caught in the rock-crushing at the national level? I'm just so amazed that these gals fight like they do. It's so enervating."

November, 1972

Vaginal Politics

We have lived through the era when happiness was a warm puppy, and the era when happiness was a dry martini, and now we have come to the era when happiness is "knowing what your uterus looks like." For this slogan, and for what is perhaps the apotheosis of the do-it-yourself movement in America, we have the Los Angeles Self-Help Clinic to thank: this group of women has been sending its emissaries around the country with a large supply of plastic specula for sale and detailed instructions on how women can perform their own gynecological examinations and abortions. Some time ago, two of its representatives were in New York, and Ellen Frankfort, who covers health matters for the *Village Voice,* attended a session. What she saw makes the rest of the women's movement look like a bunch of old biddies at an American Legion Auxiliary cake sale:

"Carol, a woman from the . . . Clinic, slipped off her dungarees and underpants, borrowed somebody's coat and stretched it out on a long table, placed herself on top, and, with her legs bent at the knees, inserted a speculum into herself. Once the speculum was in place, her cervix was completely visible and each of the fifty women present took a flashlight and looked inside.

" 'Which part is the cervix? The tiny slit in the middle?'

" 'No, that's the os. The cervix is the round, dough-nut-shaped part.' "

Following the eyewitness internal examination, Carol and her colleague spoke at length about medical ritual and how depersonalizing it is, right down to the drape women are given to cover their bodies; they suggested that women should instead take the drape and fling it to the ground. If the doctor replaces it, they suggest throwing it off again. And if he questions this behavior (and one can only wonder at a doctor who would not), they recommend telling him that California doctors have stopped draping. "And if you're in California, tell him that doctors in New York have stopped this strange custom." The evening ended with a description of the most radical self-help device of all: the period extractor, a syringe-and-tube contraption that allows a woman to remove her menstrual flow, all by herself, in five minutes; if she is pregnant, the embryo is sucked out instead. Color slides were shown: a woman at home, in street clothes, gave herself an early abortion using the device. "I hesitate to use the word 'revolutionary,'" Frankfort wrote of the event, "but no other word seems accurate. . . ."

Ellen Frankfort's report on this session is now reprinted as the opening of her new book, *Vaginal Politics* (Quadrangle Books). When I first read it in the *Voice,* I was shocked and incredulous. At the same time, it seemed obvious that at the rate things were going in the women's movement, within a few months the material would not be surprising at all. Well, it has been over a year since the Los Angeles Self-Help Clinic brought the word to the East, and what they advocate is as shocking and incredible as ever. I mean, it's awfully perplexing that anyone would suggest throwing linens all over an examination room when a simple verbal request would probably do the trick. And when Frankfort informs us, as she does at the end of her book, that "there are several groups of women who get together in New York City and on their dining room tables or couches look at the changes in the cervix," it is hard not to long for the days when an evening with the girls meant bridge.

On the other hand . . .

On the other hand, the self-help movement and the concern with health issues among women's groups spring from a very real and not at all laughable dissatisfaction with the American medical establishment, and most particularly with gynecologists. In New York, the women's movement has turned this dissatisfaction to concrete achievement in placing paid women counselors in major abortion clinics and in working to lower rates and change procedures at these clinics; in Boston, the Women's Health Collective has produced a landmark book, *Our Bodies, Our Selves,* a comperhensive compilation of information about how the female body works. But the animosity against doctors has also reached the point where irresponsibility, not to mention hard-core raunchiness, has replaced reason. When Frankfort asked Carol about the possible negative effects of period extraction, her question was taken as a broad-scale attack on feminism. The fact is that if doctors were prescribing equipment as untested as these devices are, equipment which clearly violates natural body functions, the women's health movement would be outraged. It has been justifiably incensed that birth-control pills were mass-marketed after only three years' observation on a mere 132 women. The Los Angeles women are advocating a device that has not been tested at all for at-home use; in hospitals, it has been used safely, but by doctors, and primarily for early abortion. There is a horrifying fanaticism to all this, and it springs not just from the zeal to avoid doctors entirely, but from something far more serious. For some time, various scientists have been attacking women's liberation by insisting that because of menstruation, women are unfit for just about everything several days a month. In a way, the Los Angeles women are supporting this assertion in their use of period extraction for non-abortion purposes; what they are saying, in effect, is, yes, it *is* awful, it is truly a curse, and here is a way to be done with it in five minutes. I am not one of those women who are into "blood and birth and death," to quote Joan Didion's rather extraordinary and puzzling definition of what it means to be female, but I do think that the desire to eliminate the first of these functions springs from a self-hate that is precisely parallel to the male fear of blood that underlies so many primitive taboos toward women.

In any event, the extremist fringe of the self-help movement in no way invalidates the legitimate case women have against gynecologists. These doctors are undoubtedly blamed for a great deal that is not their fault; they are, after all, dealing in reproductive and sexual areas, two of the most sensitive and emotionally charged for women. Still, I have dozens of friends who have been mis-diagnosed, mis-medicated, mistreated and misinformed by them, and every week, it seems, I hear a new gynecological atrocity tale. A friend who asks specifically not to be sedated during childbirth is sedated. Another friend who has a simple infection is treated instead for gonorrhea, and develops a serious infection as a side effect of the penicillin. Another woman tells of going to see her doctor one month after he has delivered her first child, a deformed baby, born dead. His first question: "Why haven't you been to see me in two years?" Beyond all this, there are the tales of pure insensitivity to psychological problems, impatience with questions, preachy puritanism particularly toward single women, and, for married women, little speeches on the need to reproduce. My usual reaction to these stories is to take a feminist line, blame it all on complicated sexism or simple misogyny. But what Ellen Frankfort has managed to do in *Vaginal Politics*—and what makes her book quite remarkable—is to broaden women's health issues far beyond such narrow analyses. "The mystique of the doctor, profound as it is, is not the only negative feature of the present health system," she writes. "Unfortunately, the women from the Los Angeles Self-Help Clinic . . . seemed to be focusing mainly on this aspect of the problem while ignoring the need for institutional change. Feminist politics cannot be divorced from other political realities, such as health care and safety."

The problems women face with doctors stem not just from their own abysmal lack of knowledge about their bodies, and not just from female conditioning toward male authority figures. (The classic female dependency on the obstetrician, Frankfort notes, transfers at childbirth to dependency on the pediatrician, all this "in perfect mimicry of the dependency relationship of marital roles.") They stem also from inequities in the health system and from the way doctors are educated. The brutalizing, impersonal training medical students receive prepares them perfectly to turn around and treat their patients in exactly the same way: as infants. Writes Frankfort: "We feel hesitant to question their procedures, their fees or their hours, and often we're simply grateful that we're able to see them at all, particularly if they're well recommended." My sister-in-law, who is pregnant, told me the other day that she was afraid to bother her gynecologist with questions for fear of "getting on his wrong side." As Frankfort points out: "The fear that a patient will be punished unless he or she is totally submissive reveals a profound distrust of the people in control of our bodies." (I have, I should point out, exactly the same fears about my lawyer, my accountant, and my maid. Generally speaking, none of us is terribly good at being an employer.)

Vaginal Politics covers a wide range of health subjects: the New York abortion scene, drugs, psychoanalysis, breast cancer, venereal disease, the law, the growth of the consumer health movement in America. At times, the tone is indignant to the point of heavy-handedness. Also, I caught several factual errors. But Frankfort has written with contagious energy and extraordinary vitality; without exaggeration, her book is among the most basic and important written about women's issues, and I hope it will not be overlooked now that the more faddish women's books have had their day.

The tendency in reviewing this book, of course, is to stress the more outlandish and radical aspects of the health movement, but Frankfurt's real strength lies in her painstaking accumulation of political incidents. There is the case of Shirley Wheeler, who had an abortion and was convicted for manslaughter under an 1868 Florida law. The condition of her probation: marry the man she lives with, or return to her parents in North Carolina. If she refused, if she, for example, lived instead with a woman, her parole would be rescinded and she would be sent to jail. There are the guidelines for sterilization proposed by the American College of Obstetricians and Gynecologists: no woman can be sterilized unless her age multiplied by the number of children she has borne is 120 or more. Writes Frankfort: "The logic behind this sliding scale of reproductive output has it that in order to earn her right to not have children, a woman must first produce some." For men, under the same guidelines, voluntary sterilization is available to anyone over twenty-one. Period. Another incident in the book, and one that is particularly compelling, is the case of Dr. Joseph Goldzieher, who is at the Southwest Foundation for Research and Education in San Antonio, Texas. Some years ago, Dr. Goldzieher got to wondering whether one reason birth-control pills prevent conception might simply be psychological, and he decided to run a test to see. There were 398 women, most of them Chicanos, coming to the clinic, and one fifth of them were given placebos instead of contraceptives. Within a year, six of the women, all mothers of at least three other children, had given birth. Writes Frankfort: "The ethics of a researcher who considers an unwanted child an unfortunate 'side effect' of an experimenter's curiosity needs no further commentary. However, what should be pointed out . . . is that not only does Dr. Goldzieher work at a research institute where poor nonwhite women are selected for experimentation, but he is also a consultant to several drug companies. In fact, the experiment was sponsored by Syntex, a leading pill manufacturer. . . ."

And so the doctors work for the drug companies and prescribe accordingly, the hospitals take advantage of the poor, the laws are antiquated, it goes on and on. Knowing what your uterus looks like can't hurt, I suppose, and knowing more about your body can only help, but it seems a shame that so much more energy is being directed into this sort of contemplation and so little into changing the political structure. There is a tendency throughout the movement to overindulge in confession, to elevate The Rap to a religious end in itself, to reach a point where self-knowledge dissolves into high-grade narcissism. I know that the pendulum often has to swing a few degrees in the wrong direction before righting itself, but it does get wearing sometimes waiting for the center to catch hold.

December, 1972

Bernice Gera,
First Lady Umpire

Somewhere in the back of Bernice Gera's closet, along with her face mask and chest protector and simple spiked shoes, is a plain blue man's suit hanging in a plastic bag. The suit cost $29 off the rack, plus a few dollars for shortening the sleeves and pants legs, but if you ask Bernice Gera a question about that suit —where she bought it, for example, or whether she ever takes it out and looks it over—her eyes widen and then blink, hard, and she explains, very slowly so that you will not fail to understand, that she prefers not to think about the suit, or the shoes, or the shirt and tie she wore with it one summer night last year, when she umpired what was her first and last professional baseball game, a seven-inning event in Geneva, New York, in the New York–Pennsylvania Class A League.

It took four years for Bernice Gera to walk onto that ball field, four years of legal battles for the right to stand in the shadow of an "Enjoy Silver Floss Sauerkraut" sign while the crowd cheered and young girls waved sheets reading "Right On, Bernice!" and the manager of the Geneva Phillies welcomed her to the game. "On behalf of professional baseball," he said, "we say good luck and God bless you in your chosen profession." And the band played and the spotlights shone and all three networks recorded the event. Bernice Gera had become the first woman in the 133-

year history of the sport to umpire a professional base-ball game.

I should say, at this point, that I am utterly baffled as to why any woman would want to get into profes-sional baseball, much less work as an umpire in it. Once I read an article in *Fact* magazine that claimed that men who were umpires secretly wanted to be moth-er figures; that level of idiotic analysis is, as far as I am concerned, about what the game and the profes-sion deserve. But beyond that, I cannot understand any woman's wanting to be the first woman to do any-thing. I read about those who do—there is one in today's newspaper, a woman who is suing the State of Colorado for the right to work on a team digging a tunnel through the Rocky Mountains—and after I get through puzzling at the strange desires people have, awe sets in. I think of the ridicule and abuse that wom-an will undergo, of the loneliness she will suffer if she gets the job, of the role she will assume as a freak, of the smarmy and inevitable questions that will be raised about her heterosexuality, of the derision and smug satisfaction that will follow if she makes a mistake, or breaks down under pressure, or quits. It is a devastat-ing burden and I could not take it, could not be a pioneer, a Symbol of Something Greater. Once I was the first woman to deposit $500 in a bank that was giving out toasters that day, and I found even that an uncomfortable responsibility. The point of all this, though, is Bernice Gera, and the point of Bernice Gera is that Bernice Gera failed to play out the role. In her first game, she made a mistake. And broke down under pressure. And couldn't take it. And quit. Which was not the way it was supposed to happen: instead, she was supposed to have been tougher and stronger and better than any umpire in baseball and end up a grim stone bust in the Cooperstown Hall of Fame. Bernice Gera turned out to be only human, after all, which is not a luxury pioneers are allowed. At the time, I thought it was all hideously ironic and even a little funny; a few months later, I got to wondering what had really happened and what was happening to Mrs. Gera now, now that she had blown her modest deferred dream.

Bernice Gera lives in a three-room walk-up apartment in Queens. In it there is a candle shaped like a softball, an ashtray shaped like a mitt, a lighter shaped like a bat, a crocheted toaster cover shaped like a doll wearing a baseball cap, an arrangement of dried flowers containing a baseball, powder puffs, and a small statue of Mickey Mouse holding a bat. On the wall is a very large color photograph of Mrs. Gera in uniform holding a face mask, and a few feet away hangs a poem that reads: "Dear God, Last night I did pray/That You would let me in the game today./And if the guys yell and scream,/Please, God, tell them You're the captain of the team." All the available shelf space is crammed with trophies and plaques; there must be forty or fifty of them, some for bowling (she averages 165) but most for baseball, for her career on a women's softball team in Detroit, and for her charity batting exhibitions against people like Roger Maris and Sid Gordon. "I can hit the long ball," she says, and she can, some 350 feet. There is also a framed clipping of an old Ripley's Believe It Or Not, a syndicated feature that has come a long way since the days when it printed items that were remotely unbelievable. "Believe It Or Not," it reads, "a New York City housewife has won 300 large dolls for needy youngsters living at the children's shelter of the Queensboro Society for the Prevention of Cruelty to Children by her skill at throwing a baseball at amusement parks."

Mrs. Gera is a short, slightly chunky woman who wears white socks and loafers; her short blondish-brown hair is curled and lacquered. Around her neck is a gold charm decorated with a bat, mitt, and pearl baseball which she designed and had made up by a local jeweler. Her voice is flat and unanimated, unless, of course, she is talking about baseball: she can describe, exultantly, one of the happiest days of her life, when she had a tooth extracted and was able to stay home from work to see the Pirates win the World Series in 1960. Bernice Gera is, more than anything, a fan, an unabashed, adoring fan, and her obsession with baseball dates back to her childhood, when she played with her older brothers on a sandlot in the Pennsylvania mining town where she was raised. "I have loved, eaten, and lived baseball since I was eight years old," she says. "Put yourself in my shoes. Say you loved baseball. If you love horses, you can be a jockey. If you love golf or swimming, look at Babe Didrikson and Gertrude Ederle. These are great people and they had an ability. I had it with baseball. What could I do? I couldn't play. So you write letters, begging for a job, any job, and you keep this up for years and years. There had to be a way for me. So I decided to take up a trade. I decided to take up umpiring."

In June, 1967, Mrs. Gera enrolled as a student at the National Sports Academy in West Palm Beach, Florida, a school run by an old-timer named Jim Finley for ballplayers and umpires. The Associated Press sent a reporter to cover Mrs. Gera's education, and Finley said she was coming along just fine. "She had the habit of carrying on conversations with the players," said Finley, "but we broke that by giving her push-ups. . . . I had expected a tomboy when she signed up, but Bernice is every bit a girl." A few months after her graduation from the Academy, magna cum laude, Mrs. Gera commented good-naturedly on her experience there. "I didn't have too much trouble," she said. "The chest protector didn't fit very well. Those things aren't made for women. And the players tried to give me a hard time." (Little jokes about Mrs. Gera's chest protector were to become the leitmotif of her saga.) Years passed before Mrs. Gera confessed that the school had actually been a nightmare. "It was a horrible, lonely experience," she said. "They all thought there was something wrong with me." At night, in the dormitory, the men threw beer cans and bottles at her bedroom door. On the field, the players hazed her, threw extra balls into the game during a play, spit tobacco juice on her shoes, cursed to try to shake her up. She would call a runner safe and he would snarl, "Bad call. I was out." Said Mrs. Gera: "When you begin, you take an awful lot of abuse. They make you, to prepare you for the future. I think they overdid it with me. Tobacco juice. That was unnecessary. It all hinged on whether I could take it. I took it. But after, I'd go home and cry like a baby."

A diploma in umpiring was worth nothing at all when it came to getting a job, and so in 1968 Mrs. Gera began the first of several lawsuits against professional baseball. Her lawyer, who served without fee, was a New York politician named Mario Biaggi, who called press conference after press conference to announce action after action. Finally, in 1969, Mrs. Gera was given a contract by the New York–Pennsylvania Class A League promising her $200 in wages, $300 in expenses, and five cents a mile for a month, beginning with a twilight doubleheader August 1. The sports pages were full of pictures of Mrs. Gera, thumbs up, victorious. But on July 31, the president of the National Association of Professional Baseball Leagues invalidated the contract by refusing to sign it. Mrs. Gera was heartbroken, but she confined her reaction to a string of sports metaphors: "I guess I just can't get to first base. . . . It's a strikeout but I will come up again. The game is not over."

The lawsuit continued. There was a hearing at the New York State Human Rights Commission, where George Leisure, attorney for the baseball interests, said that Mrs. Gera was publicity mad and that furthermore she did not meet any of the physical requirements for being an umpire. Umpires, he said, should be five feet ten inches tall, and weigh 170 pounds. "Being of the male sex is a bone-fide qualification for being a professional umpire," said Leisure. In November, 1970, the Human Rights Commission held that the National League discriminated not only against women but against men belonging to short ethnic groups and would have to "establish new physical standards which shall have a reasonable relation to the requirements of the duties of an umpire." The League promptly appealed the decision, and the legal process dragged on.

Maury Allen of the New York *Post* went into the locker room of the New York Mets at one point during Mrs. Gera's years in chancery and asked some of the ballplayers how they felt about her. He recorded, in response, a number of attempted witticisms about her chest protector, along with a predictable but nonetheless interesting series of antediluvian remarks. "I read the stories about her and she said that she expected people would call her a 'dumb broad,'" said Jerry Koosman. "Hell, that's the nicest thing people would call her. What do you think she'd hear when a batter hit a line drive off a pitcher's cup?" Said Ron Swoboda: "She'd have fifty guys yelling at her in language she wouldn't believe. If she heard those dirty words and didn't react, then they would have to give her a hormone test."

Bernice Gera waited almost two years for the State Court of Appeals to uphold the Human Rights Commission ruling; finally, in the spring of 1972, she once again signed a contract with the New York–Pennsylvania League. In late June, having allowed to reporters that she was "grateful to God and grateful to baseball," she drove to Geneva, New York, for her début. There was a banquet Thursday night and she was cheered over roast chicken. She was ecstatic. "I was in baseball," Mrs. Gera recalled. "I can't tell you. I was on top of the world. And then, the bubble burst."

On Friday, there was a meeting of the League umpires. "That meeting," Mrs. Gera said. "It was like, if you had a group of people in a room and they just ignored you. How can I express it? They made it ob-

vious they didn't want me. How would you feel?
You're supposed to work your signals out with your
partner. You're a team. You have to know what he's
going to do. But my partner wouldn't talk to me. I
sat there for six hours. A lot of other things went on
that I don't want to discuss because I'm going to write
about it someday. I should have realized if they fought
me in court they weren't going to welcome me, but I
never thought they would do that to me. That was the
only way they could get to me, through the other umpires. If they won't work with you, you can't make
it."

Saturday night, when Bernice Gera walked out onto
the field in her $29 suit, she had come to a decision.
She would leave baseball if her fellow umpire would
not tell her his signals. Her partner, a lanky young
man named Doug Hartmayer, who was also making
his professional début, refused even to acknowledge her
presence. But the crowd loved her, applauded her em-
phatic calls, and was amused by her practically
perpetual motion. Then, in the fourth inning, a member of the Auburn Phillies came into second base and
Mrs. Gera, in an uncharacteristically unemphatic move,
ventured a safe call. Seconds later, she realized he was
out in a force play, and brought her fist up. The manager of the Auburn team, Nolan Campbell, who had
said before the game that Mrs. Gera was "going to
have one heck of a time taking the abuse," ran out
onto the field and begin to shout and chase after
her. She ejected him from the game. Campbell was
furious. "She admitted she made a mistake," he said
later. "I told her, that's two mistakes. The first one was
putting on a uniform."

When the game ended, Bernice Gera, trailed by camera crews and a dozen reporters, strode into the
clubhouse and announced, "I've just resigned from
baseball." Then she wheeled around, left the field, and
burst into tears in the back of a friend's car. NBC's
Dick Schaap asked Doug Hartmayer how he felt about

her quitting. "I was glad," said Hartmayer. "Her job wasn't bad except she changed that call at second base, which is a cardinal sin in baseball." As Schaap later noted, "She committed the cardinal sin of baseball—she admitted she made a mistake."

It is hard to believe that things would not have worked out had Bernice Gera hung in there, stayed on, borne up somehow. It is hard to believe, too, that she could not have been helped by some real support from the women's movement. In any event, Mrs. Gera and the movement did not join forces until three weeks after her debacle, when she attended a meeting at the grubby New York headquarters of the National Organization for Women. "I'm happy to be here with all you girls—I mean women," said Mrs. Gera, and plunged into her new rhetoric. She spoke of the "calculated harassment by the sexist operators who control baseball." She hinted at a boycott of the game. She defended changing her call, quoting from the *Baseball Manual,* a publication that seems to provide the messages in fortune cookies: "To right a wrong is honorable. Such an action will win you respect."

"People are saying I'm a quitter, but I'm not," she said, "not after what baseball put me through. Someone else might have quit earlier but I stayed with it. I would have shined a ballplayer's shoes. That's how much I like baseball."

And so it is over, and Bernice Gera has, if not a profession, a title. She is Bernice Gera, First Lady Umpire. That is how she signs autographs and that is how she is identified at the occasional events she is invited to attend. Bernice Gera, First Lady Umpire, modeled at a fashion show at Alexander's department store, along with several other women of achievement. Bernice Gera, First Lady Umpire, umpired a CBA softball game at Grossinger's and was third-base coach for the wives of the Atlanta Braves at an exhibition game. Bernice Gera, First Lady Umpire, sits on a couch in her Queens apartment and looks back on it all.

"People say to me, you quit," she said. "I heard some reports back that I closed the door for all women, that I put women's lib back years. How could I close a door? I was the first woman in baseball. What did I do—close doors or open doors?" It is an interesting question, really, but Bernice Gera prefers not to hear the answer or dwell on the past or deal with what actually happened. "I'm in contact with baseball all the time," she says. "Don't count me out. I expect to be in baseball next year."

January, 1973

Deep Throat

The sign on the door says "Film Productions," and it all couldn't seem blander. The receptionist is a plump, pleasant woman named Frances, who looks like any receptionist in any office. But this is not, Frances assures me, any office. "No way," she says. "I used to work at the *Catholic News*. That was interesting. Then I worked at an ad agency. We had the Rheingold account and Nat 'King' Cole used to come in all the time. That was interesting. But *this* is *really* interesting." This, as it happens, is the office which produced the most successful pornographic film in the short, recent history of mass-market pornographic films. *Deep Throat*, as I write, is currently in its twenty-second record-breaking week at "the mature World Theatre" on Times Square, and is thirty-seventh on the list of *Variety*'s top grossers, having so far taken in some $1,500,000. The film cost $40,000 to make, and its profits are such that Frank Yablans of Paramount Pictures, who speaks in sentences that sound suspiciously like *Variety* headlines, calls it "The *Godfather* of the sex pix."

I am here at the offices of Film Productions because one week ago, on one of those evenings when it was almost impossible to find a movie someone in the group had not seen, we ended up in a packed theatre watching the 7:30 show of *Deep Throat*, ended up there having read in Suzy Knickerbocker's column that Mike Nichols had seen it three times and having heard, from friends, that it was not only the best film of its kind but actually funny. *Screw* magazine had given it 100 points on the Peter Meter. There was an interview with the star of the film, one Miss Linda Lovelace, in *Women's Wear Daily*—"I'm just a simple girl who likes to go to swinging parties and nudist colonies," she said —and a column by Pete Hamill in *New York* magazine. In short, there was an overwhelming amount of conversation and column space concerning the film; not to have seen it seemed somehow . . . derelict.

The plot of *Deep Throat*—that it has one at all is considered a breakthrough of a sort—concerns a young woman, Linda Lovelace playing herself, who cannot find sexual satisfaction through intercourse. "I want to hear bells ringing, dams bursting, rockets exploding," she says. She goes to a doctor and he discovers that her problem is simply that her clitoris is in her throat. (Ah, yes, the famous clitoris-in-the-throat syndrome.) Once diagnosed, she embarks on an earnest program of compensatory behavior—I should say here that her abilities have mainly to do with the fact that, like circus sword-swallowers, she has learned to control her throat muscles to the point where she seems to have no gag reflex whatsoever—and before long, dams burst and rockets explode.

"I do not know what their reasonings were or why," Lou Perry is saying, "but every top motion-picture company in the United States has called us and asked to borrow a print for the weekend." Perry is the producer of *Deep Throat*. He is thirty-five years old, dark-haired, a bit paunchy, and until all this began to happen he was Lou Perino. He is sitting in his office at Film Productions in the midst of what passes for a crisis in the sex-pix business: Hugh Hefner's aide has just called to request a print of *Deep Throat* for Hefner's personal film collection, and all the available prints are in use. "Look," Perry is saying to a tattooed person named Vinny, who works for him, "call Fort Lee. Call Atlanta. This is a very important thing. *Playboy* is giving us a three-page spread in the February issue. We gotta find a print." There are other things on Perry's mind—one is an impending trial on the obscenity of the *Deep Throat* advertising; another is the forthcoming sequel, *Deep Throat II,* which is about to go into production with a $100,000 budget; and a third is the Los Angeles premiere of *Deep Throat,* to be held at the Hollywood Cat in two weeks, complete with searchlights and Linda Lovelace herself. "She's going to do some radio interviews out there," says Perry, "and we think maybe Johnny Carson."

Exactly what Perry was doing prior to entering the pornographic film business he prefers not to say, but he is perfectly willing to tell the story of his big break. "How I got into this," he says, "is I lent—I mean, I invested money in a company that went bankrupt that was into this. We then made two pictures. One was *Sex U.S.A.* The other was called *This Film Is All About* . . . That's right. Blank. The original title was going to be a four-letter word, but we realized no newspaper would take the ad. New York papers won't even take the word 'Sex' on movies like this. To give you a for instance, *Sex U.S.A.* in the *Daily News* was printed *Xex U.S.A.* Both these films were documentaries, about events that were happening, sex shows, interviews with people about what did they think about sex shows. *Sex* cost about twelve to fifteen thousand dollars. So far, it's grossed six hundred thousand. The way *Deep Throat* came about was we decided to do another film. We didn't want to do a documentary. There was this film, *Mona,* that we had seen. It was different. It had a story. It was done with what you would call improvisational. We thought of doing possibly the same exact thing, so we decided, let's pick out a subject.

"To be honest about it, we couldn't come up with anything too good. We were just going to do another *Mona.* Then, somehow, Jerry Damiano, the writer and director, he seen this girl at a party. I assume he got fixed up with her. And he came in the next day and he said as he was driving over the Fifty-ninth Street Bridge he was thinking of her. What she had done was fantastic. He's never seen anybody do like she did. So he thought, let's make a picture about this girl.

"We started out with a fifteen-thousand-dollar picture, and then it went up to twenty-two thousand and then thirty thousand and then we said, oh the hell with it, let's go all the way. By the time we finished, we spent forty thousand. I was very worried. How would it be accepted? Before we released it, we had a screening. Personal friends, exhibitors, sub-distributors. I tell you, I was on pins and needles as to what their reaction would be. Well, I've been to many X-rated movie screenings, but this picture—in the screening, when she first gives throat, four or five of the men in the audience said, 'Hurray,' and by the end of the sequence there were fifteen guys standing and they went into a very big applause. At that point, we knew we had a hit on our hands. *Screw* reviewed it a week before it opened and said it was the best porn film ever made. That had a lot to do with what happened. We opened up against *Cabaret* and the sequel to *Shaft,* and we outgrossed both of them."

It may be a terrible mistake to take *Deep Throat* and its success seriously. These things may just happen. Their success may not mean a thing. The publicity machine marches on, and all that. But I can't help thinking that pornography that has this sort of impact must have some significance. I have seen a lot of stag films in my life—well, that's not true; I've seen about five or six—and although most of them were raunchy, a few were also sweet and innocent and actually erotic. *Deep Throat,* on the other hand, is one of the most unpleasant, disturbing films I have ever seen—it is not just anti-female but anti-sexual as well. I walked into the World Theatre feeling thoroughly unshockable —after all, I can toss off phrases like "split beaver" with almost devil-may-care abandon—and I came out of the theatre a quivering fanatic. Give me the goriest Peckinpah any day. There is a scene in *Deep Throat,* for example, where a man inserts a hollow glass dildo inside Miss Lovelace, fills it with Coca-Cola, and drinks it with a surgical straw—the audience was bursting with nervous laughter, while I sat through it literally faint. All I could think about was what would happen if the glass broke. I always cringe when I read reviews of this sort—crazy feminists carrying on, criticizing nonpolitical films in political terms—but as I sat through the film I was swept away in a bromidic wave of movement rhetoric. "Demeaning to women," I wailed as we walked away from the theatre. "Degrading to women." I began muttering about the clitoris backlash. The men I was with pretended they did not know me, and then, when I persisted in addressing my mutterings to them, they assured me that I was overreacting, that it was just a movie and that they hadn't even been turned on by it. But I refused to calm down. "Look, Nora," said one of them, playing what I suppose he thought was his trump card by appealing to my sense of humor, "there's one thing you have to admit. The scene with the Coca-Cola was hilarious."

Exactly what Linda Lovelace did for a living before becoming the first superstar of her kind is something she prefers not to be explicit about. She will say, though, that she is twenty-one years old, from Bryan, Texas, and that she decided to come to New York almost two years ago. She had met a man she calls J.R., a former Marine, who is now her manager and who taught her the trick of relaxing her throat muscles, and the two of them set off for the big city together. "I was just going to get a job as a topless dancer or something," said Miss Lovelace. "I really didn't think what happened would happen." A few months after arriving in New York, Linda and J.R. went to a party. "J.R. met Jerry Damiano and they got to talking about what

I could do," said Miss Lovelace. "And when he saw me, he liked me and the way I looked and he got carried away. The next day he was riding to work across the Brooklyn Bridge and he decided on the whole script for the movie."

Everything that has happened to Linda Lovelace since then is kind of a goof. Making the film was kind of a goof. Its success is kind of a goof. Being recognized in public is kind of a goof. "I totally enjoyed myself making the movie and all of a sudden I'm what they call a superstar," she says. "It's kind of a goof." I am talking to Miss Lovelace long distance—she is living in Texas with J.R.—and we are having a conversation that leaves something to be desired. For instance, Linda Lovelace's idea of candor is to insist that her name really is Linda Lovelace, and her idea of a clever response to the question of whether she has any idiosyncrasies is to say, "I swallow well." As if all this were not enough, it turns out that Linda Lovelace thinks the scene with the Coca-Cola and glass dildo was even funnier than my friend thinks it is. "Actually," she says, "I think the funniest thing that happened when we were shooting was when we did that scene. They were going to shoot a little bit more, but someone said something and I started laughing and the glass dildo went flying into the air and cracked into a million pieces." I am not sure what I expected from this interview—I honestly did not expect Linda Lovelace to be Jane Fonda in *Klute,* nor did I think that she would, as a result of our conversation, see the light and leave the pornographic film business forever. On the other hand, I did not expect what is happening, which is that we seem to be spending as much time talking about me and what Miss Lovelace clearly thinks of as my problems as we are about her and what I clearly think of as her problems. As in this exchange:

"How do you feel about being recognized on the street?" I ask.

"It's kind of a goof," she says.

"But," I say, "Lou Perry told me that it made you a little nervous."

"Why should it make me nervous?"

"I don't know," I say. "I might be nervous if someone recognized me as the star of a pornographic film. Especially in the Times Square area."

"Would you be nervous," she asks, "if you walked around nude and strangers saw you?"

"Yes."

"See? I wouldn't."

Or in this exchange:

"Why do you shave off your pubic hair in the film?" I ask.

"I always do," Linda Lovelace replies. "I like it."

"But why do you do it?"

"Well," she says, "it's kinda hot in Texas."

That stops me for a second. "Well," I say, "I think it's weird."

"Weird? Why?"

"Well, I don't know anyone who does that."

"Now you do," says Linda Lovelace.

"I don't have any inhibitions about sex," she says. "I just hope that everybody who goes to see the film enjoys it and maybe learns something from it." Like what? "I don't know. Enjoys their sex life better. Maybe loses some of their inhibitions." In the meantime, Linda Lovelace is about to make the sequel. She is under exclusive contract to Film Productions and receives $250 a week when she isn't working and $10,000 plus a piece of the profits for the next film. Does she want to make regular films as well as pornographic films? "Look," she says, "you make a separation between movies and this kind of movie. To me, it's just a movie, like all other movies. Only it has some much better things in it." Like what? "Like me," says Linda Lovelace.

And there we are. Linda Lovelace, "just a simple girl who likes to go to swinging parties and nudist colonies." And me, a hung-up, uptight, middle-class, inhibited, possibly puritanical feminist who lost her sense of humor at a skin flick. It's not exactly the self-image I had in mind, but I can handle it.

February, 1973

On Consciousness-
Raising

I try to remember exactly what the lie was that I
made up to tell friends a year ago, when I joined a
consciousness-raising group. They would ask me why
I had done it, why I had gotten into something like
that—a group, an actual organized activity—and I
think what I tended to reply was that I didn't see how
I could write about women and the women's movement
without joining a group. Consciousness-raising, according to all the literature, is fundamental to the women's
movement and the feminist experience, blah blah blah;
it seemed important to me to find out just what the
process was about. I said all this as if I were joining
something educational, or something that was going to
happen to me, as opposed to something I would actively participate in. The disinterested observer, and all
that. As I say, this was a lie. The real reason I joined
had to do with my marriage.

At our first meeting, we all went around the room
explaining why each of us had come. For all intents
and purposes, all eight of us were married—the one
exception had been living with a man for several years
—and, as it turned out, we were all there because of
our marriages. Most of the women said that they hoped
the group would help them find ways to make their marriages better. Margo, who was in no better shape than
the rest of us but tended to have faith in theatrical
solutions, said that what she was interested in from the

group was mischievous pranks. When we all looked blank, she explained that what she meant by her catchy little phrase was devising experiments like putting hot fudge on your nipples to perk up your sex life. It came around to me, my turn to explain why I was there. I said that I, too, hoped that the group would help me find a way to make my marriage better, but that it was just as likely that I was looking to the group for help in making it worse.

My consciousness-raising group is still going on. Every Monday night it meets, somewhere in Greenwich Village, and it drinks a lot of red wine and eats a lot of cheese. A friend of mine who is in it tells me that at the last meeting, each of the women took her turn to explain, in considerable detail, what she was planning to stuff her Thanksgiving turkey with. I no longer go to the group, for a variety of reasons, the main one being that I don't think the process works. Well, let me put that less dogmatically and more explicitly— this particular group did not work for me. I don't mean that I wasn't able to attain the exact goal I set for myself: in the six months I spent in the group, my marriage went through an incredibly rough period. But that's not what I mean when I say it didn't work.

I should point out here that consciousness-raising was never devised for the explicit purpose of saving or wrecking marriages. It happens to be quite good at the latter, for reasons I would like to go into further on, but it is intended to do something broader and more political—"to develop personal sensitivity to the various levels and forms that the oppression takes in our daily lives; to build group intimacy and thus group unity, the foundations of true internal democracy; to break down in our heads the barrier between 'private' and 'public' (the 'personal' and the 'political'), in itself one of the deepest aspects of our oppression." Those lines are quoted from a mimeographed set of guidelines which were worked out by the New York Radical Feminists and which were read at our group's first meeting, along with a set of rules: each woman must speak from personal experience, the group has no leader, each member takes her turn going around the circle, no conclusions are to be drawn until each woman has spoken, no woman is to challenge another woman's experience. I do not have any idea of what happens in other groups. It took ours just over two hours to break every one of the rules, and just over two months to abandon the guidelines altogether.

In the beginning, none of this seemed terribly important. I loved consciousness-raising. Really loved it. The process sets off a kind of emotional rush, almost a high. There is so much confession, so much support, so much apparent sisterhood. At each meeting, we would choose a topic—mothers, success, sex, femininity, and orgasms were a few we took on at the start—and it was really like being part of a novel unfolding, as every week the character of each woman became clearer and more detailed. There were tears. There were what seemed like flashes of insight. There were cast changes: two women dropped out of the group because their husbands insisted they do so; there were two new members. It all seemed heady, and fun, and yes, voyeuristic, and after every meeting I think each of us felt a kind of pride and relief, not the kind you're supposed to feel, some sort of high-principled feminist consciousness or other—we never had that—but the well-I'm-not-as-bad-off-as-I-thought sort of feeling. Women who were making it with their husbands only once or twice a week found there were women who made it with their husbands only once or twice a month. And so forth.

In the autumn, 1972, *American Scholar* there is a panel discussion on women by several notable women writers, followed by a far more interesting commentary by Patricia McLaughlin in which she mentions consciousness-raising. The problem with it, she says, "is that discoveries are made, yes. ('You feel that way? I thought only *I* felt like that.') But what is one to do with them? Discoveries have reverberations. A new idea about oneself or some aspect of one's relation to others unsettles all one's other ideas, even the super- ficially unrelated ones. No matter how slightly, it shifts one's entire orientation. And somewhere along the line of consequences, it changes one's behavior." All that may well have happened in Patricia McLaughlin's group, but it did not happen in mine. No one's be- havior changed; quite the opposite occurred. It almost seemed as if our patterns were reinforced through the group process. The tendency among us was always to side with the woman in the group against her husband, to refuse to see the part both partners usually play in marital problems, to refrain even from asking the woman what *she* might be doing to make things diffi- cult. And as for the discoveries—ah, the discoveries, guaranteed or your money back—even those had very little impact. In a different time or a different place or under different circumstances, things might have worked out exactly as they're supposed to. Three or four years ago, say—it must have been electrifying for women to get together and find, for example, that none of them could deal well with anger, or that few of them were having vaginal orgasms, or whatever. In Dubuque, say—perhaps in places like that, when housewives meet for this sort of thing, discoveries pop faster than corn, and women who have never worked go out and find jobs, women who have never shared household duties refuse to wash the dishes, or some such. Had we been single, say, or completely happy with our marriages. . . . But we were all married, living in New York, in 1972. We had read the movement literature. Almost all of us had careers. We were much too sophisticated—or so we thought—to waste time discussing hard-core move- ment concepts like "the various levels and forms that the oppression takes in our daily lives." What we wanted to talk about was men.

And so, ultimately, it all settled into a running soap opera, with new episodes on the same theme every week. Barbara and Peter, Episode 13 of the Barbara Is Uninhibited and Peter Is a Drag Show: this week Barbara and Peter went to a party and Barbara pulled down her pants and mooned the guests and Peter was furious. Joanna and Dave, Episode 19 of the Will Joanna Ever Get Dave to Share the Household Duties Show: this week Joanna refused to get out of bed and change the channel and Dave hit her and she threatened to kill herself. Claire and Herbie in the Claire Has Sexual Boredom but Loves Her Husband Show: this week a man in the office Claire has the hots for put his hand on her leg while they were having a drink at P. J. Clarke's, but it was time to go home and feed the children and she never did find out whether it was significant or an accident. And there was also me, with a brand-new episode in my series; and week after week, I felt more and more support from the group and more and more despair about a solution.

A couple of weeks ago, I went to hear Midge Decter speak before the Women's National Book Association. Decter has just published a long, almost unreadable attack on women's liberation and she has been justifiably creamed for it by the critics. The audience at the W.N.B.A. was no more responsive to her, and one of the women in it, in what I suspect was an attempt to make Decter lose even more of her credibility than she already had, asked her what she thought of consciousness-raising. "Consciousness-raising groups are of a piece with a whole cultural pattern that has been growing up," Decter replied. "This pattern begins with the term 'rapping'—which is a process in which people in groups pretend that they are not simply self-absorbed because they are talking to each other." There was a long hiss on that line, but it did not stop Decter. "I personally know of three marriages that broke up because of consciousness-raising," she said.

A year ago, I would have joined the general disdain that greeted that remark. Even now, it kills me to admit that anything Midge Decter says might just possibly be true. But I'm afraid she has a point. Unlike her, I do not consider it a blanket tragedy if a marriage breaks up; several of the marriages I know of that ended after the women entered consciousness-raising would have ended anyway; the breakups cannot really be laid to the groups, and both parties are better off. On the other hand, it seems unquestionably true that many groups tend to get into marriage counseling, and that the process itself tends to lead to exits rather than solutions. I cannot speak for anyone but myself, but it would have been crazy for my marriage to have ended; and yet, back in June, when I left consciousness-raising, it seemed more than likely.*

I suspect Decter is also on the right track when she links the process with the rap. Consciousness-raising is at the very least supposed to bring about an intimacy, but what it seems instead to bring about are the trappings of intimacy, the illusion of intimacy, a semblance of intimacy. There are incredible confidences traded, emotional moments shared, but it is all done in the context of the rap, the shut-up-it's-my-turn-now-it'll-be-yours-in-a-minute school of discussion. The case of the session on turkey stuffing is too classic an example to resist: no woman ever really wants to know what another woman is stuffing her turkey with; she just wants her turn to tell what *she* is planning to do.

What finally happened with my group—and this was, for me, by far the most serious development—was that it became an encounter group. The rules are precise on this point; consciousness-raising is *not* group therapy; there are to be no judgments, no confrontations, no challenges to another woman's experience. But, as I said, all that had begun to crumble by the end of the first meeting, when one of the women in the group

---

* I feel that a footnote is called for here, but I'm not exactly sure what to say in it. The marriage *did* end. I don't really want to go into the details of that. But I do want to make the point that when it broke up, it broke up for the right reasons. When it was over, I did not think that I was a victim, or that I-was-perfect-and-he-was-awful, or any of that.

was told by three members that her marriage sounded lousy. And I don't want to pretend that I had nothing to do with that—I was one of the three women who told her. As time went on, we all fell into the pattern. We felt free to give advice—and not friendly, gentle advice, the kind that is packed with options; this was more your I-think-you're-crazy-to-stand-for-a-minute-more-of-that kind of advice. What was especially interesting about it—and I gather this is fairly common in encounter groups—is that in spite of all this advice, none of us really wanted any one of us to get better. There was one woman in the group whose sex life was so awful that it made us all feel lucky; I think we would have been quite disturbed if she had shown up, one Monday, having straightened the whole thing out. There was another woman in the group who had what I think is called a problem about hostility. She seemed compelled, at every session, to vent her anger against some member of the group. Both these women were playing definite roles for the group, and someone with training and understanding of group dynamics might have helped them—and us—by pointing this out. But none of us was equipped to do that, and there were no controls whatsoever on anything that happened at the meetings. I am not sure that even with a leader, encounter therapy works; without a leader, it is dangerous.

In June, when our group disbanded for the summer, I left it and went into therapy again. I am not going to write a tribute to therapy here. All I can say is that I was fortunate, I found a brilliant woman therapist, and at the moment I think that things might work out. At the same time, I don't mean to write a wholesale attack on consciousness-raising. I hear of more and more groups every day, and some I hear about sound wonderful. They seem to follow the rules, they give women a real and new sense of pride, they help them change in important ways, they have to do with feminism and politics and the movement as well as with personal trauma. Mine didn't. My group thought the process could be used for something for which it was never intended. And that is the main point I want to make.

March, 1973

Dealing with the, uh, Problem

Leonard Lavin simply does not understand what all this is about.

Leonard Lavin is the kind of man who believes, almost to the point of religious fervor, in the free-enterprise system. In capitalism. In advertising. In this great land of ours. When Leonard Lavin sits in his Melrose Park, Illinois, factory, in the shade of a 75-foot-high can of Alberto VO5 hair spray, he knows that what he surveys is not just good but positive proof that America works. In less than twenty years, he has taken Alberto-Culver, a piddling drug company with sales of $300,000 a year, and brought it to its current yearly volume of $182 million. Leonard Lavin is proud of this, proud of every bit of it, and one of the things he is proudest of is the fact that there is a product on the market, a product that did not exist seven years ago and probably would not exist today but for him, and that product is going to gross over $40 million this year. Forty million dollars a year added on to the gross national product. Leonard Lavin deserves a medal for that. Right? And what he is getting instead is flak.

Leonard Lavin simply does not understand.

I will try to keep this from becoming gamy, but it is going to be hard. This is an article about the feminine-hygiene spray, and how it was developed and sold. I will try to keep it witty and charming, but inevitably something is going to sneak in to remind you what this product is really about. This product is really about vaginal odor. There are a lot of advertisements on television for the product that are so subtle on this point that some people—maybe not *you*, but some people—might not even know what the product *does*. There are a lot of men who manufacture the product who are so reluctant to talk straight about it that you can spend hours with them and not hear one anatomical phrase. They speak of "the problem." They speak of "the area where the problem exists." They speak of "the need to solve the problem." Every so often, a hard-core word slides into the conversation. Vagina, maybe. Or sometimes, from someone particularly candid or scientific, a vulva or two. But mostly, the discussion of this product from industry spokesmen is vague, elusive, euphemistic. Here, for example, are the words of Larry Foster, a public-relations man for Johnson & Johnson, manufacturers of Vespré and Naturally Feminine. He is speaking here of feminine-hygiene sprays and cunnilingus; I tell you this for the simple reason that he does not.

"What we're talking about here," said Foster, "is first, sex, and second, that segment of sex and how you react to it. Whether or not one needs something like this . . ." He paused. "If you were to really get people honest in terms of their reaction, the reaction is not with the product but with deep-seated feelings, not about sex, but that segment of sex." Another pause. "In terms of body odor, feminine odor, in terms of that, each man would give you a difference of opinion, ranging from acceptance of it or disdain of it. Some people would consider it a problem. Others would say, 'What the hell's the difference whether you spray or not?' I don't know why I wax eloquent, but I do think everyone's missing the point."

All this vagueness and euphemism is entirely appropriate, of course, since the name of the product itself is a total euphemism. The feminine-hygiene spray is the term coined by the industry for a deodorant for the external genital area (or, more exactly, the external perineal area). The product has been attacked continuously since its introduction in 1966—by women's liberationists, who think it is demeaning to women; by consumerists, who think it is unnecessary; and by medical doctors, who think it is dangerous. In spite of the widely shared belief among these groups that the product is perhaps *the* classic example of a bad idea whose time has come, and in spite of the product's well-publicized involvement in the recent hexachlorophene flap, the feminine-hygiene spray appears to be here to stay. It is currently being manufactured by more than twenty companies (one industry source claims to have seen some forty different brands) and being used by over twenty million women, and this, according to those in the industry, is just the beginning. Says Steve Bray, who is in charge of Pristeen at Warner-Lambert Company: "It will be as common as toothpaste."

In a time when the young are popularly assumed to be, if not the great unwashed, at least free from the older generation's absurd hang-ups about odors, the sprays are selling most briskly to teen-agers and women in their early twenties. "Secretaries and stewardesses," says the clerk at Manhattan's Beekhill Chemists, which cannot keep the products in stock and which has been having a run of late on a corollary product, the raspberry douche called Cupid's Quiver. Secretaries and stewardesses. It figures. Scratch any trend no one you know is into and you will always find secretaries and stewardesses. They are also behind Dr. David Reuben, contemporary cards, *Jonathan Livingston Seagull,* water beds, Cold Duck, Rod McKuen, and Minute Rice.

"American women are pushovers for this product," says Dr. Norman Pleshette, a New York gynecologist. "I think it comes down to menstruation, which many are taught is unclean. There are euphemisms for it, like The Curse. This is something instilled in women from girlhood on." Adds Dr. Sheldon H. Cherry, another New York gynecologist: "It's capitalizing on a small minority of women's fears and sensitivities about odors in this area. The average woman certainly does not need the routine use of a feminine deodorant. And women who do have odors should see a gynecologist to see if there is a pathological cause."

The success of the feminine-hygiene spray provides a fascinating paradox in that its manufacturers have taken advantage of the sexual revolution to sell something that conveys an implicit message that sex—in the natural state, at least—is dirty and smelly. To make matters more complicated, these same manufacturers are oblivious to the paradox: in their eyes, the mere fact that the sprays are being marketed is a breakthrough, a step forward in the realm of sexual freedom, a solid thrust in the never-ending fight against hypocrisy and puritanism. We didn't invent the problem, they say. It has always been there. The feminine-hygiene spray has just come along to save the day. "Somewhere out there," says Jerry Della Femina, whose advertising agency did the campaigns for Feminique, "there is a girl who might be hung up about herself, and one day she goes out and buys Feminique and shoots up with it, and she comes home and that one night she feels more confident and she jumps her husband and for the first time in her life she has an orgasm. If I can feel I was responsible for one more orgasm in the world, I feel I deserve the Nobel Peace Prize."

How Alberto-Culver Tests FDS for Effectiveness (A Short but Gamy Section)

A housewife comes to the Institute for Applied Pharmaceutical Research in Yeadon, Pennsylvania, on a Monday morning, at which time she is evaluated by direct olfaction on a scale of eight. What this means, in plain language, is that she simply takes off her clothes, lies down on a bed with a curtain and sheet completely covering the upper half of her body, and a judge takes a nosepiece, places it over her vulvar area, and sniffs. The judge is female, earns up to $1,000 a week, and works also in underarm odor. The housewife is scored: from 0 to 2 means little or no odor; 3–4 denotes a detectable odor though one that is of no concern to the subject; 5–6 is strong odor; and 7–8 is ripe. After the first evaluation, the housewife takes a bath using only soap and water. Six, twelve, and twenty-four hours later, she is sniffed by the judge and evaluated. On Tuesday, the process is repeated. Wednesday and Thursday, she is sprayed with FDS after bathing and the evaluation proceeds. During the four-day period, the housewife sleeps at home but is not allowed to have intercourse. She receives $150 for four days of work. According to the Institute, the test shows that FDS reduces feminine odor more effectively than soap and water—by 74–78 percent after six hours, 53–59 percent after twelve hours, and 38–40 percent after twenty-four hours.

The first feminine-hygiene spray was a Swiss product called Bidex, which was introduced by Medelline in Europe in the early 1960s. Technologically, the product was a step forward: until that point, all sprays had been the wet, sticky variety; the Swiss were the first to use a propellant called fluorocarbon 12 to produce a warm, dry spray. The American rights to Bidex were purchased by Warner-Lambert, which imported it and put it into a small test market under its original name. At the same time, Leonard Lavin, president of Alberto-Culver, saw Bidex during a 1965 trip through Europe, and he brought the concept back to his company and summoned his chief scientist, John A. Cella. Before coming to Alberto-Culver, Cella was part of the original research team on the birth-control pill at G. D. Searle; once, while working with the raw estrogen used in Enovid, he sprouted a pair of breasts. They were only temporary. Cella is a good-natured man who seems to be thoroughly used to the enthusiasms of his boss; still, he admits that the idea of feminine sprays threw him a little. "We were all a little nonplused about it," he recalled. "Oh, well. They never look to me for marketing decisions. Mr. Lavin came back from Switzerland and said, 'This thing will go. Can we do it?' I said, 'I think we can do it.' We had some background research on this going back to 1963 in the general deodorant field, in terms of what you could deodorize. It was a toiletry, but we were going to treat it as a pharmaceutical—we realized because of the area in which it was to be used it would have to have safety experiments. It is a grooming product, not a pharmaceutical, but it was a breakthrough."

In terms of product development, the feminine-hygiene spray was not a breakthrough at all. It followed right along in the tradition of mouthwashes and underarm deodorants and foot sprays, a tradition Ralph Nader has called the why-wash-it-when-you-can-spray-it ethic. What the manufacturers of all these products have succeeded at over the years, as economist John Kenneth Galbraith points out, is in manufacturing and creating the demand for a product at the same time they manufacture and create the product. In the area of personal grooming, the new product is considerably easier to introduce than in other fields. "Year after year," says Ralph Nader, "in any industry, the sellers become very acute in appealing to those features of a human personality that are easiest to exploit. Everyone knows what they are. It's easiest to exploit a person's sense of fear, a person's sense of being ugly, a person's sense of smelling badly, than it is to exploit a person's appraisal or appreciation of nutrition, and, shall we say, less emotive and more rational consumer value."

The underarm deodorant, which was the first product to capitalize on the American mania for odor suppression, was introduced over a hundred years ago, in

1870. A few years later, Mum, the first trademark brand, came onto the market. It had a primitive formula of wax which was intended to stop perspiration by simply plugging pores. In 1914, Odo-Ro-No, with a base of aluminum chloride, became the first nationally advertised brand, and it was followed by dozens of products containing metal-salts bases, which did control perspiration though they were less successful in controlling odor. The big deodorant boom came in the late 1940s, when the less than euphonious term "B.O." was coined, and in the 1950s, when hexachlorophene came onto the market. This drug, which its manufacturers claim inhibits the growth of microorganisms on skin surfaces and thus prevents odors, was discovered in 1939 by a scientist named Dr. William Gump and became the sole property of the New York-based Givaudan Corporation, which sold it by the trainload to the manufacturers of Dial Soap, PhisoHex (the soap used in hospitals by doctors and nurses before surgery), and a wide variety of deodorant products. In the 1960s, the introduction of the aerosol container clinched hexachlorophene's domination of deodorant formulas for the reason that alternative agents, like aluminum salts, could not be used in metal cans. Right Guard, and other "family-type" products, zoomed to the top of sales charts. At the same time, the mouthwash manufacturers introduced pocket-sized spray atomizers, and the first foot-spray powders came onto the market. The American woman had been convinced to spray her mouth, her underarms, and her feet; the feminine-hygiene spray, at this point, was probably inevitable.

Q: Miss Provine, why are vaginal deodorant sprays becoming so popular?

A: I believe that we're living in a wonderful new era. An era where femininity really counts. And the more feminine you feel, the more feminine you'll be. The hygiene sprays are popular because they're an ex-

*tension of this feeling. It tells me that we've come a
long way since the horrible days when women were
ashamed of feeling like women.*
                                    —Advertisement for Feminique.

Dorothy Provine, in this case, happens to be right.
Women *have* come a long way since the horrible days
when women were ashamed of feeling like women. To
be exact, women have come full circle. Leonard
Lavin is fond of reminding his critics that the tradition
for the feminine-hygiene spray goes back to Biblical
times; he is absolutely accurate; and he is furthermore
totally unaware that he is basing his defense of his
product on thoroughly primitive practices, purification
rites that originated from physiological ignorance and
superstition and that were instrumental in the early
forms of discrimination against women. Says Rabbi Ira
Eisenstein, editor of the *Reconstructionist* magazine:
"To take an ancient concept and apply it to a modern
one, especially for commercial purposes, to tie it in with
exalted notions, is pure exploitation and misleading."

Early purification rites surrounded the menstrual
period, which was a mysterious phenomenon: the female of the species was able to bleed without pain,
and elaborate religious customs were devised to cope
with this incredible happenstance. The most complicated and widespread of these rites followed childbirth.
"Women after childbirth," writes J. G. Frazer in *The
Golden Bough,* "are more or less tabooed all the world
over." Adds the *New Schaff-Herzog Encyclopedia of
Religious Knowledge*: ". . . in childbirth the cause of
uncleanness is not the fact of giving birth but the condition resulting which resembles that of the menses."

The assumption that women and their sexual organs
are by nature unclean is reflected in widespread practices in primitive societies. Many of these prevailed up
to this century and would be quite ludicrous if they
were not so barbaric. Delaware Indian girls, for exam-

ple, were secluded upon their first period, their heads wrapped so they could not see, and were forced to vomit frequently for twelve days; after this, they were bathed, put into fresh clothes, and secluded for two months more; at this point, they were considered clean and marriageable. The Delawares were hardly unique among American Indians: the Pueblos believed a man would become sick if he touched a menstruating woman, and the Cheyennes painted young girls red at puberty and isolated them for four days. In Morocco, menstruating women were forbidden to enter granaries or handle bees. Many Australian and New Guinea tribes forbade menstruating women to look at cattle or at the sun; one stray glimpse, it was believed, could cause milk stoppage, crop failure, plagues, famine, and total disaster.

The purification rites developed by the early Jews are probably the most commonly known today, largely because they are preserved in the Book of Leviticus. In Biblical times, menstruation was regarded as an impurity (it still is by Orthodox Jews) and women were forbidden to enter the Temple or to have intercourse at any time during menstruation and for a week thereafter. Any person who touched a woman—or even her bed linens—during her menstrual period was also considered unclean. After her period ended, the Jewish woman was required to take a ritual bath, or *mikvah,* and this was also required to cleanse objects considered idolatrous, and men who had masturbated or had had nocturnal emissions. There are Jewish theologians who insist that because men as well as women were required to bathe, the purification rites were not innately discriminatory; however, the status of women in Biblical times can be measured by the childbirth purification ritual in the Book of Leviticus (xii), which holds that a woman who bears a son is unclean for forty days thereafter, whereas a woman who bears a daughter is unclean for sixty-six days.

*As the party goes on people leave Ann alone. And
she doesn't know why. Ann is never at a loss for conversation. It's something else that makes people slowly
move away. Something that Norforms could stop right
away. What are Norforms? Norforms are the second
deodorant—a safe internal deodorant.*

—Advertisement for Norforms.

Once the basic formula for its feminine-hygiene
spray was settled on (almost all the spray formulas
contained hexachlorophene as the active deodorizing
ingredient, perfume, an emollient, and a propellant),
Alberto-Culver's research department, under Dr. Cella,
went to work testing the safety of the product. Because the spray was classified by the Food and Drug
Administration as a cosmetic, very little testing was
actually required: an eye-irritation test, an oral-toxicity
test, and a skin-patch test would have been adequate.
To its credit, Alberto-Culver went further; as it happens, though, by the standards set by its own chief
scientist, it did not go nearly far enough. In an article
on deodorants published last year in *American Per-
fumer & Cosmetics,* Cella itemized the testing he
thought was necessary for the sprays, as follows: "Animal skin irritation and sensitization studies, animal vulvar irritation studies, animal vaginal instillation studies
using the aerosol concentrates, human repeated insult
patch tests on intact and abraded skin, sub-acute and
chronic human-use tests, particle size analysis of the
spray, and animal inhalation studies." Cella wrote that
efficacy tests would also be desirable, but he added in a
sentence that is a masterpiece of scientific writing:
"Efficacy testing in this category presents problems of
delicacy which do not encumber the underarm counterparts." Prior to its introduction of FDS in late 1966,
Alberto-Culver conducted only three of these tests. One
proved that FDS did no injury to the labia and vaginas of twenty rats over a three-day period. A second
was a skin-patch test on sixty-seven persons. The third

was a use test: thirty-one women were given the product to use at home over a five-week period and showed no irritation.

In the meantime, the market-research and advertising departments of Alberto-Culver were at work developing packaging, fragrance, and a name for the spray. "The first piece of research we did in 1966," said Henry Wittemann, vice-president in charge of advertising services, "was a concept test on the product. If you did it today, there would be different results because today the category exists. The first test we commissioned said that the concept was not appealing, and based on that the research agency recommended that we drop the project. But if you looked at the research carefully, there was a suggestion that women weren't telling the interviewers what they really thought. The question came up as to whether women don't really want to talk about this subject to anyone. We had done a questionnaire about deodorants with a concept statement saying that a leading manufacturer of toiletries was planning to come out with a deodorant for the vaginal area. Do you think you need it? Would you use it? When? With a test like this, you're looking for over seventy percent to express interest. If you don't get that, chances are you don't have a product that's appealing to the market. So we decided to go to a research company that had done work in this area, a company that had done questionnaires for feminine-hygiene manufacturers like Kimberly-Clark and Johnson & Johnson. These companies know how to structure questionnaires that deal with that subject to elicit a true response. So we did that, went out with a concept statement and samples, and the interest was over seventy-eight percent. We knew we had a viable concept." Wittemann claims that at no time during this period was the question of sexual attitudes explicitly explored; the product, he claims, was conceived of as a general deodorant, not a sexual enhancer. (Sexually, the sprays are something of a bust: they cannot be used right before intercourse because they tend to cause skin irritation under those circumstances; furthermore, at least one of the sprays causes numbness of the tongue.)

"We considered names like Caresse and Care," Wittemann continued, "all the names that might be in good taste. But every name we thought fit the product belonged to another product. We were using the code name 'FD Number One,' for feminine deodorant Number One. When we were blocked, we just went to the letters 'FSD.' Then it turned out we had to choose 'FDS' because even the letters 'FSD' were taken." One criticism of FDS in recent years has been that its name is so close to F.D.A., a coincidence that might seem to imply government approval. Did that issue ever come up? "Never," Wittemann replied. "The only thing that did come up was an objection by one of our executives, who thought the name sounded too much like FDR."

"I had no idea it would be so controversial," says Leonard Lavin today. "As we developed the product and the research proved to us that there was a need for this product—both from the clinical and consumer viewpoint—we were convinced of what we had. We realized that going to the marketplace with a feminine-hygiene deodorant was not the easiest thing in the world. This was an area, after all, where other products advertised with a certain amount of reluctance. Kotex and Tampax, for example. We leaned over backwards in delicacy, elusiveness, even in design of the package: it was as soft and delicate as possible. If you looked at the first print ads, you would really have to look to find out what the product really did."

FDS was introduced on December 1, 1966. It came in a pale blue and white can, with a lacy white pattern surrounding the label. The drugstore display unit contained a sign, duplicating the first magazine advertisements, that read, "This new product will become as essential to you as your toothbrush." In smaller print:

"FDS The name is FDS. Feminine Hygiene Deodorant Spray. It is new. A most personal sort of deodorant. An external deodorant. Unique in all the world. Essential on special days. Welcome protection against odor—every single day. FDS. For your total freshness."

Ten Very Personal Questions
1. Does a woman need more than an underarm deodorant?
Yes. A woman, if she's completely honest about it, realizes her most serious problem isn't under her arms. . . .
                                —Advertisement for FDS, 1968.

With the exception of Bidex, the Swiss product Warner-Lambert still had in test market in two cities, FDS had the feminine-hygiene-spray field to itself for almost a full year. The drug trade, which is notoriously unadventurous, did not believe there was any chance for the product to succeed. Leonard Lavin, who thrives on the notion of his relatively small company as a little guy plugging away in an industry of giants, believed implicitly in FDS, and he spent hundreds of thousands of dollars animating his belief, advertising in print media, publishing pamphlets for drugstore displays, creating a demand for the product by making women understand how much they needed it. "I don't call it creating guilt," said Lavin. "That's your word. I think of what we did as raising consciousness. That's a less loaded word." There were almost daily battles to be fought: drugstore owners would not stock the item; magazines like *Life, McCall's,* and *Seventeen* were reluctant at first to accept ads for it; television had a ban on advertising for all such products. But by late 1967, Alberto-Culver had sold almost $4 million worth of sprays, and Warner-Lambert, a company that could read sales charts as well as any, decided to move ahead. The name Bidex was changed to Pristeen and the product went into a wide test-market pattern prior to national introduction in 1968. "The name Bidex was already taken under trademark," said Guido Battista, associate director in charge of research and development on toiletries and cosmetics at Warner-Lambert. "But I would have objected to it because of the possibility of misusing the product. It might have seemed to have been intended for internal use. Interestingly enough, some of the information that got to the lay people was that these were vaginal sprays, which they're not."

"Our whole approach," said Warner-Lambert's Steve Bray, "was, women have a vaginal-odor problem and here is a product that will solve the problem. They do, you know. And panty hose contribute to it. Women's liberation says that advertising is creating a need that isn't there. They say it's a nice, natural smell. That's their right. But I would go back and ask them, do women have a vaginal-odor problem? I keep going back to the problem. The problem is there."

Exactly how much of a problem American women were aware of before the sprays were introduced is not clear; what is clear is that feminine-hygiene-spray manufacturers cannot be accused of inventing it. In 1968, a market-research firm hired to investigate consumer reaction to the product gathered a group of housewives for a tape-recorded session that is notable for its embarrassment and coyness about the vaginal area. Said one woman: "I think the new deodorant sprays are sensational. Not that I have a problem down *there,* but sometimes I think I might." Said another: "I prefer sprays to the foams or powders. . . . The sprays eliminate having to touch yourself."

Says Natalie Shainess, a New York psychoanalyst: "Our society has tended since medieval times, when the odor of the great unwashed was everywhere, to work at eliminating unpleasant aspects of smell. The sense of smell is tied up with paranoia—one of the classic paranoid symptoms is the feeling, 'I smell bad. That's why no one likes me.' The sense of being mal-

odorous is connected with more serious disturbances.
These products further paranoid feelings in women and
in men about women—and the way they're advertised presents a horrendous image, of women being
inherently smelly creatures. It undermines the sense of
self and ego even as it's supposed to do something
about it."

By 1969, the market for the sprays had grown to
$19.3 million and manufacturers were tumbling in. The
boom in sales came largely because Alberto-Culver
had succeeded in getting the National Association of
Broadcasters to change its code and permit the sprays
to be advertised on television. (The stations themselves
exerted pressure, of course.) The ads were required to
be totally bland and unspecific—the word "vagina" is
not allowed on the air—and they were. A woman
walked down the beach with her child. Or lit the candles for dinner. Or talked, haltingly, about this somewhat mysterious product, she, uh, really liked a lot.
Dorothy Provine emerged from what she calls semi-
retirement to endorse Feminique, and returned to semi-
retirement $100,000 richer. The advertising budgets
backing the product mushroomed: in 1970, FDS,
which sold somewhere around $13–14 million worth
of the $32 million spray market, spent $3.5 million advertising it.

What was printed in magazine and newspaper ads
for the sprays was a good deal more blunt than what
was on television. Demure, for instance, offered this:
"You don't sleep with Teddy Bears any more." And
"Your Teddy Bear loved you no matter what." Feminique's early print ad read: "Now that 'The Pill' has
freed you from worry, 'The Spray' will help make all
that freedom worthwhile." FDS, in a more subtle ad,
nonetheless promised similar sexual rewards: "Being
close was never nicer . . . now is the Age of FDS."
Manufacturers who were unwilling to allude to sexuality stressed the importance of including the product
as part of the normal deodorant regimen. Said Pristeen,

in an ad uncannily similar to an earlier FDS ad: "Unfortunately, the trickiest deodorant problem a girl has *isn't* under her pretty little arms." Or this, from FDS: "Having a female body doesn't make you feminine. It's the extra things you do—like FDS." And yet another from FDS, this one utilizing the tried-and-true approach to upward mobility: "Could you be the last woman to be using just one deodorant?" Pristeen sought out famous women to write articles about women, with Pristeen advertisements tacked onto the end: Suzy Knickerbocker, Angie Dickinson, Mary Quant, and Judith Crist were among them. (For this, Mrs. Crist, along with Dorothy Provine, was chosen Sweet Pea of the Year by *Esquire*'s 1971 Dubious Achievement Awards.)

"The reason I did that ad had absolutely nothing to do with Pristeen," said Judith Crist, the film critic. "It was extremely naïve of me and it was two years ago and I'm ashamed to admit I'm that naïve. They were doing a two-page spread that would have eight pictures of me taken by Richard Avedon, with a two-page headline saying 'Today's Woman.' Then I had approximately eight hundred words to write what I wanted to say about women. I decided to write about women in communications. In the final column, there was a cutoff line and about four inches of space, and then it said something like, 'The modern woman who chooses to be immaculate will use Pristeen, a feminine-hygiene deodorant.' It was going to run in eight women's magazines in one month. It boggled the mind. You were reaching a hundred and twenty-five million people, an audience you couldn't reach even if you were a movie for television. Then there were the photographs with Avedon and the negatives were mine if I wanted them—which was the kind of sitting you could never otherwise afford. And then came a huge fee in addition, and I saw my son getting an extra inning in camp, redoing the living room." The fee for the ad was $5,000.

"What did bother me," Mrs. Crist went on, "was the idea of it being a vaginal deodorant. So I consulted some friends. They said, 'Boy are you ever being sexist. If it were Bond Bread, you'd do it. College presidents do commercials for the right Scotch. Why because it is a feminine-hygiene spray—what difference is a mouthwash from a vaginal wash? This is small, unenlightened thinking if we're going to get silly about vaginas.' But the essential thing was, *I* didn't say, in the ad, 'If you want to be a modern woman, use Pristeen.' What I was saying had nothing to do with Pristeen. Well, it was the dumbest decision I've ever made. It was as if I had waltzed out like Dorothy Provine and said, 'Have you used this marvelous vaginal spray?' Which I hadn't. I thought I would get responses about what I had said about women in the media—to hell with the money, the Avedon pictures, *what I said*. Instead, I got tied up with the spray. There were so many gags I could have thrown up. The students in one of my witty classes gave me an enormous box with a can of Pristeen at the bottom. The *Esquire* thing, which was quite embarrassing. Then Rex Reed, feeling betrayed because of my review of *Myra Breckinridge,* retaliated with thorough justification and said, 'Now when she walks down the aisle, people will think, Does She Or Doesn't She.' Which obliged me to retaliate. I got right down to those lower depths, which was the worst part.

"But it was a very educational experience. If Mrs. Gandhi or Golda Meir had posed for a *Playboy* foldout, the results could not have been as bad. It was a learning experience. At my age you don't think you have those."

The first hint from the critics that the sprays might not be merely useless but actually dangerous came in

November, 1970, when a Montreal gynecologist named Bernard Davis reported in the *Journal of Obstetrics and Gynecology* that he had treated some twenty to twenty-five patients who had itching, burning sensations in the vulvar area. All of them used the sprays daily. One of the patients, a fourteen-year-old girl, developed "incredibly" swollen labia, and after being treated, the doctor reported, her clitoris and labia remained "peculiarly" abnormal. Davis's letter was answered six months later by Lawrence J. Caruso, a New York gynecologist, who claimed that he had seen many cases of irritation caused by soaps and oils but none whatsoever from the sprays. Caruso conducted a study on twenty-nine of his patients, all of whom used the sprays for six months, and no abnormalities resulted. The study, Caruso said, was conducted "at the request of one manufacturer of a feminine-hygiene-deodorant spray."

The second salvo came in a long, breezily written article in *Medical Aspects of Human Sexuality* in July, 1971. In it, Bernard Kaye, an Illinois gynecologist, announced that "the great American persuader has struck again!" and went on to report that several of his patients who used the sprays had developed vulvitis; the condition did not recur, he reported, when use of the spray was discontinued. "As an added dividend of the female genital cosmetic industry," Kaye concluded, "it is to be expected that physicians will be seeing *male* genital irritations in greater numbers . . . from exposure to 'Gynacosmetics' [and] . . . from the use of the masculine version of the 'private deodorant.' "

"Honey," said Bill Blass when asked to explain why his line of cosmetics included a so-called private deodorant, "if there's a part of the human body to exploit you might as well get onto it."

Hygiene sprays for men, which are known in the trade as crotch sprays, were introduced in 1970. They have never been advertised on television and today industry sources estimate that $2 million worth of them are sold a year, 5 percent of the feminine-hygiene-spray market. It is commonly assumed by women's liberationists that products that arrive on the market with the kind of minimal testing that characterized the feminine-hygiene spray would never be sold to men—the assumption here being that men, who are in charge of manufacturing and research within industry, would never exploit their fellow men as recklessly as they do women. Their argument, however true it may be in the case of the birth-control pill, does not hold where crotch sprays are concerned. Revlon, the leading manufacturer in the men's spray market, has three brands—Braggi's Private Deodorant Spray, Bill Blass's Man's Other Deodorant, and Pub Below the Belt. It put all these products into national marketing with the three tests that are required for cosmetic products sold in spray cans—the eye-irritation, oral-toxicity and skin-patch tests—plus usage tests. The skin-patch test, according to Dr. Earl W. Brauer, Revlon vice-president in charge of medical affairs, "was not done on the penis but on an area where it can't be tampered with. We do a closed-patch test. The product is kept in place under a closed patch for two days. It's a much higher concentration and we learn much more from such a provocative test." But isn't the skin of the penis different from other skin on the male body? "Yes," said Dr. Brauer. "It's thinner skin and there are more active nerve endings. No patch tests were done on the penis. It's not necessary."

The Food and Drug Administration began looking into the safety of the feminine-hygiene spray on a number of fronts in 1971. It was concerned about the use of the word "hygiene" in connection with the product. There was the general question of the safety of aerosol containers. And there were increasing reports of irritation caused by the sprays. In early 1971, the F.D.A.

asked the spray manufacturers for their complaint rates. Four manufacturers replied; their rates ranged from 0 per million packages sold, to 6, which was about standard, to 21 per million. (The product with the highest rate, Johnson & Johnson's Vespré, incidentally, contained over twice as much hexachlorophene as the other sprays. It was reformulated in mid-1971.) Any complaint rate over 5 per million is considered cause for concern by the F.D.A., but it is unlikely that the agency would have moved against the sprays on the mere grounds of effectiveness or excessive irritation. What finally caused it to take action was the increasing weight of evidence against hexachlorophene.

The earliest indication that there might be serious trouble with the drug actually occurred some six years ago at the Shriners Burns Institute in Galveston, Texas. This hospital, which treats severely burned children, opened in the spring of 1966, and in the first six months six of its patients suffered seizures. "We couldn't find any definite reason for it," said Dr. Duane Larson, chief of staff, "so we looked into our procedure, narrowed it down, and decided it might have something to do with the soap solution we were bathing them in—which was three percent hexachlorophene." Laboratory scientists at the Institute took animals—rats, guinea pigs, pigs, and dogs—and burned their backs and then washed them with a 3-percent hexachlorophene solution. Day after day, the hexachlorophene blood levels in the animals rose higher and higher, and they began to exhibit signs of neurological damage. They were irritable. They all dragged their hind legs. "We tested the cerebral spinal fluid," said Larson, "and were able to determine that hexachlorophene was in it, that it had the property of going through the blood/brain barrier. This was important —a number of drugs don't go into the brain but just stay in the bloodstream." When the animals were autopsied, their brains were extremely swollen.

"We found the same thing with the children," said

Larson. "As the blood level of hexachlorophene got higher, they would become irritable and have seizures. I remember one boy in particular who had a small burn on one thigh. He was having neurological problems. His serum level was extremely high—far too high for such a small burn. It turned out the nurse was soaking his dressing in a three-percent hexachlorophene solution to get it off.

"We also measured the hexachlorophene levels of doctors and nurses who scrubbed with soap containing hexachlorophene, and in none could we find a significant level. It seems to be all right for adults if you rinse it off. On the other hand, we do know it goes through normal skin as well as burned skin. We had a patient in Michigan—a baby was brought home from the hospital, a normal baby with no skin lesions, and the mother continued bathing the child in the three-percent hexachlorophene solution that was used in the hospital without rinsing it off. The baby had seizures."

Dr. Larson reported on the Institute's experience, and its decision to discontinue the use of hexachlorophene with burn victims, at a meeting of the American Burn Association in the spring of 1967. His findings were picked up by newspapers at the time, but within a few weeks the issue died down. Then, in 1971, three studies appeared that showed exactly what the Shriners Burns Institute had known for years. The most persuasive of the tests proved that newborn monkeys bathed in a 3-percent hexachlorophene solution for ninety days showed brain changes consisting of extreme swelling in the cerebellum, brainstem, and all the parts of the cord. The 3-percent solution was at that time used to bathe newborns at most American hospitals.

In November, 1971, Jack Walden, a public-relations man for the Food and Drug Administration, sat down with a Washington *Post* reporter and told her that the F.D.A. was looking into the dangers of feminine-hygiene sprays in connection with hexachlorophene. An article to that effect subsequently appeared in the *Post,* and Leonard Lavin of Alberto-Culver reacted to it by demanding Walden's resignation. Whether Lavin thought this would make the hexachlorophene problem go away is not certain; what is certain is that until the very end, every company that was directly affected by the F.D.A.'s concern about hexachlorophene looked upon the investigation as an incredible nuisance. Hexachlorophene was perfectly safe. Everyone knew that. No one had died. Thousands of newborns were bathed in it every day in hospital nurseries; as a result, there had been no staphylococcus outbreaks in American hospitals in years. Just because a few monkeys were brain-damaged did not mean that children would be. "We love hexachlorophene," said Alberto-Culver's Dr. Cella. "It's very valuable," said Warner-Lambert's Battista.

Leonard Lavin, for his part, accepted the hexachlorophene business as a small part of his ongoing battle. First there had been the consumerists—or, as he had referred to them in a letter, "negative-minded consumerist groups who would subject our entire economy to a Marxist purge of everything they object to." Now it was the government, interfering in the smooth processes of private industry. It was just like the cyclamate mess a few years back—there, Lavin insisted, was another perfectly harmless product taken off the market prematurely. He Xeroxed a long article by Vermont Royster in the *Wall Street Journal* which claimed that if aspirin were introduced today, the F.D.A. would ban it. He muttered frequently about Ralph Nader, who had been outspoken on the subject of the sprays. "If Ralph Nader had his way," Lavin said, "he would ban Fritos and soft drinks. I heard him say it myself." He commissioned studies to show the safety of hexachlorophene. Experts pored over medical reports about the sprays and jubilantly found errors in them. (One doctor, for example, had claimed in his article to have seen anal infections he traced to the perfume used in scented toilet paper. This was absurd, said Alberto-Culver's Cella: the scent came not from the paper but from the cardboard roll within; the perfume used never came in actual contact with the body.) Gus Kass, a vice-president of Alberto-Culver, delivered a speech in Chicago decrying the attacks on the cosmetics industry by newspapers and magazines. "All of them," said Kass, "are witches' brews of distorted facts, half-truths, or outright falsehoods. . . . What all of the critics fail to understand is that there is no substance to which some person is *not* allergic."

And so it went. There was bound to be some irritation from the feminine-hygiene sprays because there were bound to be some individuals who were allergic to them. And as to the rest of the complaints, the manufacturers said, these had nothing to do with hexachlorophene. Women using the products were simply using them wrong—not holding the spray far enough from their bodies or spraying just before intercourse, or spraying the actual vaginal area. (There were, to be sure, many reactions to the sprays that were caused by misuse; some manufacturers have recently inserted more explicit instructions in the spray kits.) As for hexachlorophene, most of the sprays contained less than one-tenth of 1 percent—and even if it could be shown that hexachlorophene was dangerous to humans, such a tiny amount would never hurt.

In December, 1971, the F.D.A. took its first action against hexachlorophene, announcing it was no longer recommending bathing of infants in a 3-percent hexachlorophene solution. A month later, when there was a staph outbreak in a New Haven hospital that had stopped using pHisoHex, the drug industry was as jubilant as it could be under the circumstances. But the F.D.A. claimed that the outbreak could not be traced to the ban and continued to move against the drug. It announced a three-part proposal: hexachlorophene would be banned from cosmetics except when it was used as a preservative; all drugs containing hexa-chlorophene would be required to carry warnings; and any drug with more than three-quarters of 1 percent hexachlorophene would be sold by prescription only. (Not until seven months later, when thirty-nine French infants died from the external use of a baby powder that contained, through a manufacturing error, 6 percent hexachlorophene, did the F.D.A. make final its over-the-counter ban on the drug.)

Feminine-hygiene-spray manufacturers could have fought the proposal at this point. But since the first reports of F.D.A. concern, sales of the product had dropped off. A January, 1972, attack in *Consumer Reports* had not helped. And so, voluntarily, all the manufacturers removed the drug from the feminine-spray formulas. Alberto-Culver replaced it with another antibacterial agent, and then refused to tell the press what it was. Warner-Lambert removed it entirely (they claimed it was used only as a preservative), and found that Pristeen continued to work exactly as it had before. The industry sat back, quietly, and consoled itself with memories of the cranberry scare. That had blown over ultimately, and this would, too. In the meantime, sales of the product, which had been expected to grow to $53 million in 1971, held firm at the $40 million mark. Still, $40 million worth of product wasn't bad. There were women out there who were loyal, who still wanted to buy. The rest of the public would forget. It always does.

Today children in kindergarten are taught the facts of human birth; biology is no longer a taboo subject. But a product that recognizes the existence of the difference between man and woman—and also happens to be relatively new—was sure to become a target in the age of consumerism and women's lib. Soap and water were good enough for grandma, but we think women have changed. Our sales and those of our competitors prove it.—From a form letter written by Leonard Lavin to customers requesting information on the safety of feminine-hygiene sprays.

Leonard Lavin simply does not understand what all this is about.

March, 1973

The Hurled
Ashtray

I once heard a swell story about Gary Cooper.
The person I heard the story from did this terrific
Gary Cooper imitation, and it may be that when I tell
you the story (which I am about to), it will lose
something in print. It may lose everything, in fact. But
enough. The story was that Gary Cooper was in a London restaurant at a large table of friends. He was sitting
in a low chair, with his back to the rest of the room,
so no one in the restaurant even knew that he was
tall, much less that he was Gary Cooper. Across the
way was a group of Teddy boys (this episode took
place long long ago, you see), and they were all mis-
behaving and making nasty remarks about a woman at
Cooper's table. Cooper turned around to give them
his best mean-and-threatening stare, but they went
right on. Finally he got up, very very slowly, so slowly that it took almost a minute for him to go from
this short person in a low chair to a ten-foot-tall man
with Gary Cooper's head on top of his shoulders.
He loped over to the table of Teddy boys, looked down
at them, and said, "Wouldja mind sayin' that agin?"
The men were utterly cowed and left the restaurant
shortly thereafter.

Well, you had to be there.

I thought of Gary Cooper and his way with words
the other day. Longingly. Because in the mail, from
an editor of *New York* magazine, came an excerpt

from a book by Michael Korda called *Male Chauvinism: How It Works* (Random House). I have no idea whether Korda's book is any good at all, but the excerpt was fascinating, a sort of reverse-twist update on Francis Macomber, as well as a pathetic contrast to the Gary Cooper story. It seems that Korda, his wife, and another woman were having dinner in a London restaurant recently. Across the way was a table of drunks doing sensitive things like sniggering and leering and throwing bread balls at Mrs. Korda, who is a looker. Her back was to them, and she refused to acknowledge their presence, instead apparently choosing to let the flying bread balls bounce off her back onto the floor. Then, one of the men sent over a waiter with a silver tray. On it was a printed card, the kind you can buy in novelty shops, which read: "I want to sleep with you! Tick off your favorite love position from the list below, and return this card with your telephone number. . . ." Korda tore up the card before his wife could even see it, and then, consumed with rage, he picked up an ashtray and threw it at the man who had sent the card. A fracas ensued, and before long, Korda, his wife, and their woman friend were out on the street. Mrs. Korda was furious.

"If you ever do that again," she screamed, "I'll leave you! Do you think I couldn't have handled that, or ignored it? Did I ask you to come to my defense against some poor stupid drunk? You didn't even think, you just reacted like a male chauvinist. You leapt up to defend *your* woman, *your* honor, you made me seem cheap and foolish and powerless. . . . God Almighty, can't you see it was none of your business! Can't you understand how it makes me feel? I don't mind being hassled by some drunk, I can take that, but to be treated like a chattel, to be robbed of any right to decide for myself whether I'd been insulted, or how badly, to have you react for me because I'm *your* woman . . . that's really sickening, it's like being a slave." Korda repeats the story (his wife's diatribe is even longer in the original version) and then, in a *mea culpa* that is only too reminiscent of the sort that used to appear in 1960s books by white liberals about blacks, he concludes that his wife is doubtless right, that men do tend to treat women merely as appendages of themselves.

Before printing the article, *New York* asked several couples—including my husband and me—what our reaction was to what happened, and what we would have done under the circumstances. My initial reaction to the entire business was that no one ever sends me notes like that in restaurants. I sent that off to the editor, but a few days later I got to thinking about the story, and it began to seem to me that the episode just might be a distillation of everything that has happened to men and women as a result of the women's movement, and if not that, at least a way to write about etiquette after the revolution, and if not that, nothing at all. Pulled as I was by these three possibilities, I told the story over dinner to four friends and asked for their reaction. The first, a man, said that he thought Mrs. Korda was completely right. The second, a woman, said she thought Korda's behavior was totally understandable. The third, a man, said that both parties had behaved badly. The fourth, my friend Martha, said it was the second most boring thing she had ever heard, the most boring being a story I had just told her about a fight my college roommate had with a cabdriver at Kennedy Airport.

In any case, before any serious discussion of the incident of the hurled ashtray, I would like to raise some questions for which I have no answers. I raise them simply because if that story were fed into a computer, the only possible response it could make is We Do Not Have Sufficient Information to Make an Evaluation. For example:

Do the Kordas have a good marriage?

Was the heat working in their London hotel room the night of the fracas?

Was it raining out?

What did the second woman at the table look like? Was she as pretty as Mrs. Korda? Was she ugly? Was part of Michael Korda's reaction—and his desire to assert possession of his wife—the result of the possibility that he suspected the drunks thought he was with someone funny-looking?

What kind of a tacky restaurant is it where a waiter delivers a dirty message on a silver tray?

What about a woman who ignores flying bread balls? Wasn't her husband justified in thinking she would be no more interested in novelty cards?

Did Michael Korda pay the check before or after throwing the ashtray? Did he tip the standard 15 percent?

Since the incident occurs in London, a city notorious for its rampant homoerotic behavior, and since the table of drunks was all male, isn't it possible that the printed card was in fact intended not for Mrs. Korda but for Michael? In which case how should we now view his response, if at all?

There might be those who would raise questions about the ashtray itself: was it a big, heavy ashtray, these people might ask, or a dinky little round one? Was it glass or was it plastic? These questions are irrelevant.

In the absence of answers to any of the above, I would nonetheless like to offer some random musings. First, I think it is absurd for Mrs. Korda to think that she and she alone was involved in the incident. Yes, it might have been nice had her husband consulted her; and yes, it would have been even nicer had he turned out to be Gary Cooper, or failing that, Dave DeBusschere, or even Howard Cosell—anyone but this suave flinger of ashtrays he turned out to be. But the fact remains that the men at the table *were* insulting Korda, and disturbing his dinner, as well as hers. Their insult was childish and Korda's reaction was ludicrous, but Mrs. Korda matched them all by reducing a complicated and rather interesting emotional situation to a tedious set of movement platitudes.

Beyond that—and the Kordas quite aside, because God Almighty (as Mrs. Korda might put it) knows what it is they are into—I wonder whether there is any response a man could make in that situation which would not disappoint a feminist. Yes, I want to be treated as an equal and not as an appendage or possession or spare rib, but I also want to be taken care of. Isn't any man sitting at a table with someone like me damned whatever he does? If the drunks in question are simply fools, conventioneers with funny paper hats, I suppose that a possible reaction would be utter cool. But if they were truly insulting and disturbing, some response does seem called for. Some wild and permanent gesture of size. But on whose part? And what should it consist of? And how tall do you have to be to bring it off? And where is the point that a mild show of strength becomes crude macho vulgarity; where does reserve veer off into passivity?

Like almost every other question in this column, I have no positive answer. But I think that if I ever found myself in a similar situation, and if it was truly demeaning, I would prefer that my husband handle it. My husband informs me, after some consideration, that the Gary Cooper approach would not work. But he could, for example, call over the captain and complain discreetly, perhaps even ask that our table be moved. He could hire a band of aging Teddy boys to find out where the drunks were staying and short-sheet all their beds. Or—and I think I prefer this—he could produce, from his jacket pocket, a printed card from a novelty shop reading: "I'm terribly sorry, but as you can see by looking at our dinner companion, my wife and I have other plans."

I'm going out to have those cards made up right now.

April, 1973

Truth and Consequences

I read something in a reporting piece years ago that made a profound impression on me. The way I remember the incident (which probably has almost nothing to do with what actually happened) is this: a group of pathetically naïve out-of-towners are in New York for a week and want very much to go to Coney Island. They go to Times Square to take the subway, but instead of taking the train to Brooklyn, they take an uptown train to the Bronx. And what knocked me out about that incident was that the reporter involved had been cool enough and detached enough and professional enough and (I could not help thinking) cruel enough to let this hopeless group take the wrong train. I could never have done it. And when I read the article, I was disturbed and sorry that I could not: the story is a whole lot better when they take the wrong train.

When I first read that, I was a newspaper reporter, and I still had some illusions about objectivity—and certainly about that thing that has come to be known as participatory journalism; I believed that reporters had no business getting really involved in what they were writing about. Which did not seem to me to be a problem at the time. A good part of the reason I became a newspaper reporter was that I was much too cynical and detached to become involved in anything;

I was temperamentally suited to be a witness to events. Or so I told myself.

And now things have changed. I would still hate to be described as a participatory journalist; but I am a writer and I am a feminist, and the two seem to be constantly in conflict.

The problem, I'm afraid, is that as a writer my commitment is to something that, God help me, I think of as The Truth, and as a feminist my commitment is to the women's movement. And ever since I became loosely involved with it, it has seemed to me one of the recurring ironies of this movement that there is no way to tell the truth about it without, in some small way, seeming to hurt it. The first dim awareness I had of this was during an episode that has become known as the *Ladies' Home Journal* action. A couple of years ago, as you may remember, a group of feminists sat in at the offices of *Journal* editor John Mack Carter to protest the antediluvian editorial content of his magazine; to their shock, Carter acceded to their main demand, and gave them ten pages of their own in the *Journal,* and $10,000. Shortly thereafter, I was asked if I would help "edit" the articles that were being written for the section—I put edit in quotes, because what we were really doing was rewriting them—and I began to sit in on a series of meetings with movement leaders that I found alternatingly fascinating, horrifying, and hilarious. The moment I treasured most occurred when the first draft of the article on sex was read aloud. The article was a conversation by five feminists. The first woman to speak began, I thought, quite reasonably. "I find," she said, "that as I have grown more aware of who I am, I have grown more in touch with my sexuality." The second woman—and you must remember that this was supposed to be a conversation—then said, "I have never had any sensitivity in my vagina." It seemed to me that the only possible remark a third person might contribute was "Coffee, tea or milk?" —there was no other way to turn it into a sensible exchange. Anyway, when the incident happened, I told it to several friends, who all laughed and loved the story as much as I did. But the difference was that they thought I was telling the story in order to make the movement sound silly, whereas I was telling the story simply in order to describe what was going on.

Years pass, and it is 1972 and I am at the Democratic Convention in Miami attending a rump, half-secret meeting: a group of Betty Friedan's followers are trying to organize a drive to make Shirley Chisholm Vice-President. Friedan is not here, but Jacqui Ceballos, a leader in N.O.W., *is,* and it is instantly apparent to the journalists in the room that she does not know what she is talking about. It is Monday afternoon and she is telling the group of partisans assembled in this dingy hotel room that petitions supporting Chisholm's Vice-Presidential candidacy must be in at the National Committee by Tuesday afternoon. But the President won't be nominated until Wednesday night; clearly the Vice-Presidential petitions do not have to be filed until the next day. I am supposed to be a reporter here and let things happen. I am supposed to let them take the wrong train. But I can't, and my hand is up, and I am saying that they must be wrong, they must have gotten the wrong information, there's no need to rush the petitions, they can't be due until Thursday. Afterward, I walk out onto Collins Avenue with a fellow journalist/feminist who has managed to keep her mouth shut. "I guess I got a little carried away in there," I say guiltily. "I guess you did," she replies. (The next night, at the convention debate on abortion, there are women reporters so passionately involved in the issue that they are lobbying the delegates. I feel slightly less guilty. But not much.)

To give you another example, a book comes in for review. I am on the list now, The Woman List, and the books come in all the time. Novels by women. Nonfiction books about women and the women's movement. The apparently endless number of movement-oriented and movement-inspired anthologies on feminism; the even more endless number of anthologies on the role of the family or the future of the family or the decline of the family. I take up a book, a book I think might make a column. It is *Women and Madness,* by Phyllis Chesler. I agree with the book politically. What Chesler is saying is that the psychological profession has always applied a double standard when dealing with women; that psychological definitions of madness have been dictated by what men believe women's role ought to be; and this is wrong. Right on, Phyllis. But here is the book: it is badly written and self-indulgent, and the research seems to me to be full of holes. If I say this, though, I will hurt the book politically, provide a way for people who want to dismiss Chesler's conclusions to ignore them entirely. On the other hand, if I fail to say that there are problems with the book, I'm applying a double standard of my own, treating works that are important to the movement differently from others: babying them, tending to gloss over their faults, gentling the author as if she and her book were somehow incapable of withstanding a single carping clause. *Her heart is in the right place; why knock her when there are so many truly evil books around?* This is what is known in the women's movement as sisterhood, and it is good politics, I suppose, but it doesn't make for good criticism. Or honesty. Or the truth. (Furthermore, it is every bit as condescending as the sort of criticism men apply to books about women these days—that unconsciously patronizing tone that treats books by and about women as some sort of sub-genre of literature, outside the mainstream, not quite relevant, interesting really, how-these-women-do-go-on-and-we-really-must-try-to-understand-what-they-are-getting-at-whatever-it is.)

I will tell you one more story to the point—though this one is not about me. A year and a half ago, some women from the Los Angeles Self-Help Clinic came to

New York to demonstrate do-it-yourself gynecology and performed an abortion onstage using a controversial device called the Karman cannula. Subsequently, the woman on whom the abortion had been performed developed a serious infection and had to go into the hospital for a D and C. One of the reporters covering the story, a feminist, found out about the infection, but she decided not to make the fact public, because she thought that to do so might hurt the self-help movement. When I heard about it, I was appalled; I was more appalled when I realized that I understood why she had done it.

But I cannot excuse that kind of self-censorship, either in that reporter or in myself. I think that many of us in this awkward position worry too much about what the movement will think and how what we write will affect the movement. In fact, the movement is nothing more than an amorphous blob of individual women and groups, most of whom disagree with each other. In fact, no amount of criticism of the movement will stop its forward momentum. In fact, I am intelligent enough to know that nothing I write really matters in any significant way to any of it. And knowing all this, I worry. I am a writer. I am a feminist. When I manage, from time to time, to overcome my political leanings and get at the truth, I feel a little better. And then I worry some more.

May, 1973

Baking Off

Roxanne Frisbie brought her own pan to the twenty-fourth annual Pillsbury Bake-Off. "I feel like a nut," she said. "It's just a plain old dumb pan, but everything I do is in that crazy pan." As it happens, Mrs. Frisbie had no cause whatsoever to feel like a nut: it seemed that at least half the 100 finalists in the Bake-It-Easy Bake-Off had brought something with them—their own sausages, their own pie pans, their own apples. Edna Buckley, who was fresh from representing New York State at the National Chicken Cooking Contest, where her recipe for fried chicken in a batter of beer, cheese, and crushed pretzels had gone down to defeat, brought with her a lucky handkerchief, a lucky horseshoe, a lucky dime for her shoe, a potholder with the Pillsbury Poppin' Fresh Doughboy on it, an Our Blessed Lady pin, and all of her jewelry, including a silver charm also in the shape of the doughboy. Mrs. Frisbie and Mrs. Buckley and the other finalists came to the Bake-Off to bake off for $65,000 in cash prizes; in Mrs. Frisbie's case, this meant making something she created herself and named Butterscotch Crescent Rolls—and which Pillsbury promptly, and to Mrs. Frisbie's dismay, renamed Sweet 'N Creamy Crescent Crisps. Almost all the recipes in the finals were renamed by Pillsbury using a lot of crispy snicky snacky words. An exception to this was Sharon Schubert's Wiki Wiki Coffee Cake, a name which ought to have been snicky snacky enough; but Pillsbury, in a moment of restraint, renamed it One-Step Tropical

Fruit Cake. As it turned out, Mrs. Schubert ended up winning $5,000 for her cake, which made everybody pretty mad, even the contestants who had been saying for days that they did not care who won, that winning meant nothing and was quite beside the point; the fact was that Sharon Schubert was a previous Bake-Off winner, having won $10,000 three years before for her Crescent Apple Snacks, and in adition had walked off with a trip to Puerto Vallarta in the course of this year's festivities. Most of the contestants felt she had won a little more than was really fair. But I'm getting ahead of the story.

The Pillsbury Company has been holding Bake-Offs since 1948, when Eleanor Roosevelt, for reasons that are not clear, came to give the first one her blessing. This year's took place from Saturday, February 24, through Tuesday, February 27, at the Beverly Hilton Hotel in Beverly Hills. One hundred contestants—97 of them women, 2 twelve-year-old boys, and 1 male graduate student—were winnowed down from a field of almost 100,000 entrants to compete for prizes in five categories: flour, frosting mix, crescent main dish, crescent dessert, and hot-roll mix. They were all brought, or flown, to Los Angeles for the Bake-off itself, which took place on Monday, and a round of activities that included a tour of Universal Studios, a mini-version of television's *Let's Make a Deal* with Monty Hall himself, and a trip to Disneyland. The event is also attended by some 100 food editors, who turn it from a mere contest into the incredible publicity stunt Pillsbury intends it to be, and spend much of their time talking to each other about sixty-five new ways to use tuna fish and listening to various speakers lecture on the consumer movement and food and the appliance business. General Electric is co-sponsor of the event and donates a stove to each finalist, as well as the stoves for the Bake-Off; this year, it promoted a little Bake-Off of its own for the microwave oven, an appliance we were repeatedly told was the biggest improvement in cooking since the invention of the Willoughby System. Every one of the food editors seemed to know what the Willoughby System was, just as everyone seemed to know what Bundt pans were. "You will all be happy to hear," we were told at one point, "that only one of the finalists this year used a Bundt pan." The food editors burst into laughter at that point; I am not sure why. One Miss Alex Allard of San Antonio, Texas, had already won the microwave contest and $5,000, and she spent most of the Bake-Off turning out one Honey Drizzle Cake after another in the microwave ovens that ringed the Grand Ballroom of the Beverly Hilton Hotel. I never did taste the Honey Drizzle Cake, largely because I suspected—and this was weeks before the *Consumers Union* article on the subject—that microwave ovens were dangerous and probably caused peculiar diseases. If God had wanted us to make bacon in four minutes, He would have made bacon that cooked in four minutes.

"The Bake-Off is America," a General Electric executive announced just minutes before it began. "It's family. It's real people doing real things." Yes. The Pillsbury Bake-Off is an America that exists less and less, but exists nonetheless. It is women who still live on farms, who have six and seven children, who enter county fairs and sponsor 4-H Clubs. It is Grace Ferguson of Palm Springs, Florida, who entered the Bake-Off seventeen years in a row before reaching the finals this year, and who cooks at night and prays at the same time. It is Carol Hamilton, who once won a trip on a Greyhound bus to Hollywood for being the most popular girl in Youngstown, Ohio. There was a lot of talk at the Bake-Off about how the Bake-It-Easy theme had attracted a new breed of contestants this year, younger contestants—housewives, yes, but housewives who used whole-wheat flour and Granola and sour cream and similar supposedly hip ingredients in their recipes and were therefore somewhat more sophisticated, or urban, or something-of-the-sort than your usual Bake-Off contestant. There were a few of these—two, to be exact: Barbara Goldstein of New York City and Bonnie Brooks of Salisbury, Maryland, who actually visited the Los Angeles County Art Museum during a free afternoon. But there was also Suzie Sisson of Palatine, Illinois, twenty-five years old and the only Bundt-pan person in the finals, and her sentiments about life were the same as those that Bake-Off finalists presumably have had for years. "These are the beautiful people," she said, looking around the ballroom as she waited for her Bundt cake to come out of the oven. "They're not the little tiny rich people. They're nice and happy and religious types and family-oriented. Everyone talks about women's lib, which is ridiculous. If you're nice to your husband, he'll be nice to you. Your family is your job. They come first."

I was seven years old when the Pillsbury Bake-Off began, and as I grew up reading the advertisements for it in the women's magazines that were lying around the house, it always seemed to me that going to a Bake-Off would be the closest thing to a childhood fantasy of mine, which was to be locked overnight in a bakery. In reality, going to a Bake-Off *is* like being locked overnight in a bakery—a very bad bakery. I almost became sick right there on Range 95 after my sixth carbohydrate-packed sample—which happened, by coincidence, to be a taste of the aforementioned Mrs. Frisbie's aforementioned Sweet 'N Creamy Crescent Crisps.

But what is interesting about the Bake-Off—what is even significant about the event—is that it is, for the American housewife, what the Miss America contest used to represent to teen-agers. The pinnacle of a certain kind of achievement. The best in field. To win the Pillsbury Bake-Off, even to be merely a finalist in it, is to be a great housewife. And a creative housewife. "Cooking is very creative." I must have heard that line thirty times as I interviewed the finalists. I don't happen to think that cooking is very creative—what interests

me about it is, on the contrary, its utter mindlessness
and mathematical certainty. "Cooking is very relaxing"
—that's my bromide. On the other hand, I have to
admit that some of the recipes that were concocted
for the Bake-Off, amazing combinations of frosting mix
and marshmallows and peanut butter and brown sugar
and chocolate, were practically awe-inspiring. And
cooking, it is quite clear, is only a small part of the
apparently frenzied creativity that flourishes in these
women's homes. I spent quite a bit of time at the
Bake-Off chatting with Laura Aspis of Shaker Heights,
Ohio, a seven-time Bake-Off finalist and duplicate-
bridge player, and after we had discussed her high-
protein macaroons made with coconut-almond frosting
mix and Granola, I noticed that Mrs. Aspis was wearing green nail polish. On the theory that no one who
wears green nail polish wants it to go unremarked upon,
I remarked upon it.

"That's not green nail polish," Mrs. Aspis said. "It's
platinum nail polish that I mix with green food color-
ing."

"Oh," I said.

"And the thing of it is," she went on, "when it chips,
it doesn't matter."

"Why is that?" I asked.

"Because it stains your nails permanently," Mrs.
Aspis said.

"You mean your nails are permanently green?"

"Well, not exactly," said Mrs. Aspis. "You see, last
week they were blue, and the week before I made purple, so now my nails are a combination of all three.
It looks like I'm in the last throes of something."

On Sunday afternoon, most of the finalists chose to
spend their free time sitting around the hotel and so-
cializing. Two of them—Marjorie Johnson of Robbins-
dale, Minnesota, and Mary Finnegan of Minneota,
Minnesota—were seated at a little round table just off
the Hilton ballroom talking about a number of things,

including Tupperware. Both of them love Tupperware.

"When I built my new house," Mrs. Johnson said, "I had so much Tupperware I had to build a cupboard just for it." Mrs. Johnson is a very tiny, fortyish mother of three, and she and her dentist husband have just moved into a fifteen-room house she cannot seem to stop talking about. "We have this first-floor kitchen, harvest gold and blue, and it's almost finished. Now I have a second kitchen on my walk-out level and that's going to be harvest gold and blue, too. Do you know about the new wax Congoleum? I think that's what I put in—either that or Shinyl Vinyl. I haven't had to wash my floors in three months. The house isn't done yet because of the Bake-Off. My husband says if I'd spent as much time on it as I did on the Bake-Off, we'd be finished. I sent in sixteen recipes—it took me nearly a year to do it."

"That's nothing," said Mrs. Finnegan. "It took me twenty years before I cracked it. I'm a contest nut. I'm a thirty-times winner in the *Better Homes & Gardens* contest. I won a thousand dollars from Fleischmann's Yeast. I won Jell-O this year, I'm getting a hundred and twenty-five dollars' worth of Revere cookware for that. The Knox Gelatine contest. I've won seven blenders and a quintisserie. It does four things —fries, bakes, roasts, there's a griddle. I sold the darn thing before I even used it."

"Don't tell me," said Mrs. Johnson. "Did you enter the Crystal Sugar Name the Lake Home contest?"

"Did I enter?" said Mrs. Finnegan. "Wait till you see this." She took a pen and wrote her submission on a napkin and held it up for Mrs. Johnson. The napkin read "Our Entry Hall." "I should have won that one," said Mrs. Finnegan. "I did win the Crystal Sugar Name the Dessert contest. I called it 'Signtation Squares.' I think I got a blender on that one."

"Okay," said Mrs. Johnson. "They've got a contest now, Crystal Sugar Name a Sauce. It has pineapple in it."

"I don't think I won that," said Mrs. Finnegan, "but I'll show you what I sent in." She held up the napkin and this time what she had written made sense. "Hawaiian More Chant," it said.

"Oh, you're clever," said Mrs. Johnson.

"They have three more contests so I haven't given up," said Mrs. Finnegan.

On Monday morning at exactly 9 a.m., the one hundred finalists marched four abreast into the Hilton ballroom, led by Philip Pillsbury, former chairman of the board of the company. The band played "Nothin' Says Lovin' Like Somethin' from the Oven," and when it finished, Pillsbury announced: "Now you one hundred winners can go to your ranges."

Chaos. Shrieking. Frenzy. Furious activity. Cracking eggs. Chopping onions. Melting butter. Mixing, beating, blending. The band perking along with such carefully selected tunes as "If I Knew You Were Coming I'd Have Baked a Cake." Contestants running to the refrigerators for more supplies. Floor assistants rushing dirty dishes off to unseen dishwashers. All two hundred members of the working press, plus television's Bob Barker, interviewing any finalist they could get to drop a spoon. At 9:34 a.m., Mrs. Lorraine Walmann submitted her Cheesy Crescent Twist-Ups to the judges and became the first finalist to finish. At 10 a.m., all the stoves were on, the television lights were blasting, the temperature in the ballroom was up to the midnineties, and Mrs. Marjorie Johnson, in the course of giving an interview about her house to the Minneapolis *Star,* had forgotten whether she had put one cup of sugar or two into her Crispy Apple Bake. "You know, we're building this new house," she was saying. "When I go back, I have to buy living-room furniture." By 11 a.m., Mae Wilkinson had burned her skillet corn bread and was at work on a second. Laura Aspis had lost her potholder. Barbara Bellhorn was distraught because she was not used to California apples. Alex Allard was turning out yet another Honey Drizzle Cake. Dough and flour were all over the floor. Mary Finnegan was fussing because the crumbs on her Lemon Cream Bars were too coarse. Marjorie Johnson was in the midst of yet another interview on her house. "Well, let me tell you," she was saying, "the shelves in the kitchen are built low. . . ." One by one, the contestants, who were each given seven hours and four tries to produce two perfect samples of their recipes, began to finish up and deliver one tray to the judges and one tray to the photographer. There were samples everywhere, try this, try that, but after six tries, climaxed by Mrs. Frisbie's creation, I stopped sampling. The overkill was unbearable: none of the recipes seemed to contain one cup of sugar when two would do, or a delicate cheese when Kraft American would do, or an actual minced onion when instant minced onions would do. It was snack time. It was convenience-food time. It was less-work-for-Mother time. All I could think about was a steak.

By 3 p.m., there were only two contestants left—Mrs. Johnson, whose dessert took only five minutes to make but whose interviews took considerably longer, and Bonnie Brooks, whose third sour-cream-and-banana cake was still in the oven. Mrs. Brooks brought her cake in last, at 3:27 p.m., and as she did, the packing began. The skillets went into brown cartons, the measuring spoons into barrels, the stoves were dismantled. The Bake-Off itself was over—and all that remained was the trip to Disneyland, and the breakfast at the Brown Derby . . . and the prizes.

And so it is Tuesday morning, and the judges have reached a decision, and any second now, Bob Barker is going to announce the five winners over national television. All the contestants are wearing their best dresses and smiling, trying to smile anyway, good sports all, and now Bob Barker is announcing the winners. Bonnie Brooks and her cake and Albina Flieller and her Quick Pecan Pie win $25,000 each. Sharon Schu-

bert and two others win $5,000. And suddenly the
show is over and it is time to go home, and the
ninety-five people who did not win the twenty-fourth
annual Pillsbury Bake-Off are plucking the orchids
from the centerpieces, signing each other's programs,
and grumbling. They are grumbling about Sharon
Schubert. And for a moment, as I hear the grumbling
everywhere—"It really isn't fair." . . . "After all, she
won the trip to Mexico"—I think that perhaps I am
wrong about these women: perhaps they are capable
of anger after all, or jealousy, or competitiveness, or
something I think of as a human trait I can relate to.
But the grumbling stops after a few minutes, and I find
myself listening to Marjorie Johnson. "I'm so glad I
didn't win the grand prize," she is saying, "because if
you win that, you don't get to come back to the next
Bake-Off. I'm gonna start now on my recipes for next
year. I'm gonna think of something really good." She
stopped for a moment. "You know," she said, "it's going to be very difficult to get back to normal living."

July, 1973

Crazy Ladies: I

Washington is a city of important men and the women they married before they grew up. Is that how the saying goes? Something like that, anyway. All those tidy little summations of local phenomena—California is fine if you're an orange; first prize one week in Philadelphia, second prize two weeks in Philadelphia —turn out, after close inspection, to be even more accurate than they seemed at first hearing. But the one I wanted to talk about is the one about Washington.

I don't know a great deal about life in Washington for women—I spent a summer there once working in the White House, and my main memories of the experience have to do with a very bad permanent wave I have always been convinced kept me from having a meaningful relationship with President Kennedy—but that doesn't stop me from making generalizations about the place. Because it has always seemed obvious that life for women in Washington combined the worst qualities of the South and small-town life. Washington is a city of locker-room boys, and all the old, outmoded notions apply: men and women are ushered to separate rooms after dinner, sex is dirty, and they are still serving onion-soup dip. A married woman with any brains and personality at all is faced with a Hobson's choice: she can be her husband's appendage, and pay that price—and we have Joan Kennedy as the classic example of a woman who has. Or she can be a crazy lady.

I should clarify what I mean by crazy lady. In my

youth—which ended about eight years ago—I occasionally had a date with someone who was very straight. Which is to say, square. In most relationships, I tend to be the straight one, cautious, conservative, not crossing on the Don't Walk, but whenever I was confronted with someone even squarer than I was, whenever I was confronted with a relationship where the role of the crazy person was up for grabs, I would leap in, say outrageous things, end the evening lying down in Times Square with a lampshade on my head. I wasn't a patch on Zelda Fitzgerald—I would never have leaped into the Plaza fountain for fear of ruining my hair—but I was in there doing my damnedest.

The crazy lady I have been thinking about apropos of all this is Barbara Howar. Mrs. Howar is not really crazy in any context where real craziness exists—in New York, she would just be another outspoken, somewhat bitchy woman. But Washington is a city that is an all-purpose straight man: you don't have to be a terribly funny joke to get laughs in Washington, and you don't have to be a terribly crazy person to seem about as loony as they come. Just jump into the Supreme Court fountain. Or refuse to go off with the ladies after dinner. Or have an affair. That's about all it takes.

Barbara Howar, who has written a book about her experiences in Washington, *Laughing All the Way* (Stein & Day), was a socialite who hooked up with Lynda Bird and Luci Baines in some inexplicable way having to do with wedding trousseaus and became a social light in the Johnson Administration. In an era not noted for its sophisticates, she became notorious for her sharp-tongued remarks, some of which were occasionally mistaken for wit and some of which were actually witty. Then she was dumped shortly before Luci's wedding, in a tacky and hilarious episode which confronted her with a true moral dilemma: should she warp her six-year-old daughter for life by withdrawing her from the role of flower girl in the cere-

mony, or warp her for life by letting her go on with
it? After resolving this dilemma (she let her go on
with it) and living through a decent period of social
ostracism, Mrs. Howar emerged once again to resume
her role as the town's Peck's Bad Girl.

As she recalls in her memoir, "I was filled with an
uncontrollable desire to shock—to say or do anything
that would raise voices and eyebrows or boredom's
threshold. I had a natural ability to alienate people I
found dull. I would rudely cut short any matron lady
who dwelled too long on her wonderful children, her
indispensable housekeeper, or her husband's unher-
alded political abilities. I once interrupted a woman
deep into her monologue about the great Lone Star
State with, 'If I hear one more exaggeration about Texas, I'm going to throw up on the Alamo.' I became
incautious in my description of Texas habits, asking
one gentleman sporting a hammered-silver belt studded
with ersatz stones: 'Did you make it at summer camp?'
And to a Dallas lady in reference to the Tex-Mex
delicacy she had proudly served for dinner: 'Did you
get this recipe off the back of a Fritos bag?' "

I liked *Laughing All the Way*—it happens to be far
more charming than what I just quoted would indicate;
it also happens to be fun to read. But I was surprised
to find it as fascinating as I did, because what Barbara
Howar has written, and I don't think it was uninten-
tional, is almost a case study of a kind of woman and a
kind of misdirected energy. And while I'm not sure any
lesson or moral can be drawn from it—or if it can, I'm
not about to do it—her floundering attempts to make a
life and identity for herself are genuinely, and surprisingly, moving.

Barbara Howar came to Washington just out of finishing school and the South and went to work on
Capitol Hill. She was pretty and blond and energetic
and, as we used to say in high school, popular. As she
writes, "I never wearied of flying on private planes to
the Kentucky Derby with groups that included Aly

Khan, of first nights of Broadway musicals. . . . But the tedium of clerical work dulled the excitement of my social life. I started doing bizarre things—my personal indicator of unrest—painting mailboxes shocking pink, leaping fully clothed into the Supreme Court fountain. One day I woke up disposed to do the only thing I had not yet tried: marriage." She married very well: her husband was a builder, heir to an Arab fortune, and she entered into the life of being his wife, working at charities, being photographed at luncheons, having parties and a family. Then 1964 came along, and because it was the thing to do that year, she went to work for the campaign of President Johnson.

It is altogether possible that had Barbara Howar married someone she was more capable of being an appendage of, none of what followed would have happened. Or it would have happened much later. In any event, she went off as Lady Bird Johnson's hairdresser on the campaign swing of the South, met a Johnson aide with whom she had an affair, and charmed the President to the point that he was soon holding her hand (and falling asleep) during White House movie screenings and whirling her about the dance floor at State functions. "I was *that* woman dancing with *the* President. . . ," Mrs. Howar recalls. "It never occurred to me that I could distinguish myself in more admirable fashion." *Women's Wear Daily* began to follow her everywhere, *Life* magazine profiled her, and Maxine Cheshire watched as she danced on a table top in a white dress with gold chains she said "cut into my tender young flesh . . . just a little number the Marquis de Sade whipped up for me. . . .

"There simply was no shutting me up. I had to tell every newspaper and magazine that Mrs. Johnson, a lady who spent every waking minute planting trees in ghettos and sprinkling tulip bulbs around settlement houses that had no plumbing, was 'off base' with her Beautification Program, that it was 'like buying a wig when your teeth are rotting.' I had to say in print that Mrs. Johnson's rich New York friends 'would be better advised to donate their money to countless endeavors like fighting street crime, and that to celebrate their philanthropy I would gladly wear a bronze plaque saying: TODAY I WAS NOT RAPED OR MUGGED THROUGH THE KIND GENEROSITY OF THE LASKER/LOEB FOUNDATIONS.' "

The affair with the Johnson aide continued and became a full-fledged Washington scandal; she left her husband and went off with her lover for a week in Jamaica. "In the sultry, alien surroundings of the Caribbean," she writes, in one of the more melodramatic sections of the book, "harsh reality became larger than my fantasy of finding peace by changing marriages. I became morbidly depressed for the first time in my life. I missed the children, my home, everything familiar and comfortable. I was melancholy and homesick, maudlin in my confusion, I wanted something to make me happy, something to give me reason not to care that half my life was over and that I had no real zest for finishing out the rest. Guilty and restless as before, I saw the future now as even more menacing. I wanted it all and I wanted out. It was the woman's primal feeling of being trapped, unable to live without marriage because it was all I knew, but incapable of projecting myself happily into more of the same. My anxieties grew. I had doubts about who I was and what I wanted to be. Why was I even in Jamaica?" At about this moment, Mrs. Howar's reveries were interrupted by a group of detectives, who burst in on her and the Johnson aide, ripped the strap on her nightgown, and took pictures. Mrs. Howar returned to Washington, reconciled for a time with her husband, and was promptly dropped by the Johnsons.

At this point, Barbara Howar's story became a morality tale. Her son gets spinal meningitis and almost dies. She finally leaves her husband. She develops a social conscience through a relationship with Bobby Darin, the singer, and becomes a star on a local television news show, where her standard operating procedure was to fling her newly acquired set of facts on life in the slums at her guests. "It was a long while," she writes, "before I learned that if there was anything worse than a bigoted keeper of the status quo, it was a recycled socialite with a newly aroused public conscience." Mrs. Howar complains, in what are straight women's movement terms, that her remarks on the air were not taken seriously because she was a woman. "If my male counterparts made strong critical statements, they were 'blunt' or 'forceful'; similar candor from television women is 'cutting,' 'catty,' and 'bitchy.' " She is right about the problems—though probably not in her own case. A typical moment in Mrs. Howar's television career was this remark, made as a criticism of the space program's all-white personnel: "If N.A.S.A. can train a monkey to operate the controls of a rocket, they can train a black man."

Laughing All the Way ends with a description of Mrs. Howar's disastrous and final experience in television, cohosting a show with Mrs. David Susskind, and a marvelous chapter on her mother's death. "I am enormously saddened to understand that I would not be on my way to real peace if my mother were still alive," she writes. I don't know whether she is on her way to real peace—I would like to have heard a little more about that—but she *has* written a pretty good book about Barbara Howar. Which is more than I can say about her friend Willie Morris, who has also written a book about Barbara Howar this year, a novel called *The Last of the Southern Girls*. There is a point to be made here about borrowing material, and there is another point to be made about fact and fiction and the difference between them, but I don't want to get into that. I do want to say that I read Morris's book when I was almost finished with this column, and I note that we make some of the same points about Washington and women. I also note that he has the quote right. Washington is a city of men and the women they married when they were young. That's how it goes.

August, 1973

The Pig

Every so often, you turn a corner and Life, or the times, or the public-relations mechanism that makes the world go round throws out a hero you have to live with for a while. The point here is not about heroes but heroines. And long before the Bobby Riggs–Margaret Court tennis match took place near San Diego in May, 1973, it was clear to me that Margaret Court, the heroine who had been thrown not just my way but at the entire female population of the world, was going to leave something to be desired. The symbolism of the match was haywire enough to begin with—Riggs has always played a woman's game, Court a man's—and it was to get even more muddled before the actual confrontation. But beyond that, it seemed quite likely that of all the big women players now on the circuit, Margaret Court would be the one least likely to come through. I'm not just talking about winning the match —although God knows that would have helped. But there were the nerves. Margaret had nerves. Muscle spasms under pressure. She, of course, insisted they were simply magnesium deficiencies and potassium deficiencies; everyone else insisted they were nerves. *Just like a woman.* And then there was her style. I suppose it's not really fair to bring up style; style has nothing to do with tennis, nothing to do with anything really, but it mattered to me. I mean here is Bobby Riggs, the Lip, the hustler, saucy Bobby Riggs with his dyed red hair and his never-ending monologue and his relentless promotions (the copper-bracelet promotion, the Head tennis-clothes promotion, the 415-vitamin-pills-a-day promotion, the land-development-that-sponsored-the-match promotion, the building-project-where-Bobby-lived promotion); here is Bobby Riggs, clown prince of the Old Boy tennis circuit, great copy, and he is standing on the court of the San Vicente Country Club in San Diego Country Estates posing for photographers with Margaret Court. It is Friday afternoon, two days before the Mother's Day match, and he is whispering to Margaret, taunting her about the weight of the tennis balls and the question of her nerves and the despicable quality of women's tennis and the pressure of having all the women counting on her on Sunday. And here is Margaret. Nervous. Smiling uneasily. Occasionally offering a demure reply to Bobby or the press. "I like a challenge," she is saying. "I love the game. It's been very good to me." Like that. I didn't want *that*. I wanted some lip. I wanted some aggression. I wanted some fight. I wanted satisfaction. And what I got, what all of us got instead, was a lady.

It all began a little over two years ago, when former Wimbledon champion Bobby Riggs made a few derogatory comments about women's tennis in *Sports Illustrated* and issued a challenge to Billie Jean King: "You insist that top women players provide a brand of tennis comparable to men's. I challenge you to prove it. I contend that you not only cannot beat a top male player but that you can't beat me, a tired old man." As it happens, Billie Jean King did not say precisely that; what she did say was that women's tennis was more entertaining than men's, and that women deserved equal prize money. "Women play about twenty-five percent as good as men," Riggs countered, "so they should get about twenty-five percent of the money men receive." Nothing much came of Riggs's initial challenge, but this year Tony Trabert, the pro at San Diego Country Estates, prodded Riggs to try again, and after Mrs. King turned him down, he sent telegrams chal-

lenging six other top women players and offering
$5,000 of his own money and $5,000 put up by the
land-development corporation to the winner. Margaret
Court was first to respond. "I'd still rather play Billie
Jean," Riggs said later, "because she's really the ring-
leader of the liberation movement. She's the revolutionary. Margaret Court is such a nice person—I don't
want to say by contrast." Margaret Court, thirty years
old, Australian, mother of a fourteen-month-old boy,
is such a nice person by contrast that she doesn't even
think women deserve the same prize money as men.
"I don't feel there's a depth in the women's game," she
said. "There are so many good men. There are only six
or eight good women. If you have a thirty-two-draw
tournament, you're going to give some youngester a
thousand dollars to lose in the first round, and she
doesn't deserve it. I don't think it's good for the game.
The money will come. The depth will come. At the
moment, we're rushing it a little."

Margaret Court trained for the match in Berkeley,
working out quietly with her coach, a South African
named Dennis Van der Meer. Occasionally reporters
would come to the court for an interview and she
would reluctantly grant one. Her answers were short
and genteel; she was visibly uncomfortable with the
press. "Margaret really doesn't enjoy this," her husband, Barry, would explain. Meanwhile, every day,
Riggs played five sets, jogged two miles, swallowed 415
vitamin pills, and gave out interviews. Hundreds of
interviews. Any reporter who called or showed up got
more than he came for. "This is so much fun," Riggs
said during one interview, "that I wish it were post-
poned so we could go on like this another six weeks."

By the weekend of the match, Riggs had worked his
remarks into a finely honed performance, with set lines
that varied only slightly from press conference to press
conference. "This," he would announce, in a wonder-
fully unsyntactical sentence, "is the match of the
century between the battle of the sexes." When even

that description seemed inadequate, he would shout, "This is the most important match ever played in tennis!" After the match, he concluded at the top of his lungs that he had just played the most significant sporting event of all time. He would stand, or sit, surrounded by sports reporters, and spin a simple question into a thirty-minute monologue, inserting rhetorical questions to stretch it out, waving his copper bracelet in the air for a plug or dropping in a remark about "beautiful San Diego Country Estates." The delivery would begin slowly, usually with his old-person routine ("I'm a fifty-five-year-old man with one foot in the grave"), heavily studded with a series of impotence jokes ("The flesh won't do what the mind tells it to," and "Why shouldn't they let me into the women's tournaments —everyone knows there's no sex after fifty-five"). Then Riggs would build, gradually, ignore interrupting questions, pitch his high voice even higher, and suddenly he would be speaking so quickly that no one could quite get it down or get a word in. A typical Riggs monologue, this one recorded in the Los Angeles *Times,* went like this:

"It's pretty fantastic to think I am playing the match of the century and the battle of the sexes. This match is going to be more important than the Wimbledon, Forest Hills, or a fifty-thousand-dollar match between Laver and Rosewall. Why? Because Margaret Court is carrying the banner for women all over the world and I'm carrying the banner for all the old guys who have always felt superior to women, and they'll want to see an old guy win because then they'll feel superior, too, and I'll be doing a very good thing for all the men all over the world and they won't give in to the women's lib quite so easily. She's got twenty-five years on me. She's bigger, stronger, more agile. She's got better shots. Does everything better on a tennis court. She's the best woman player in the world. What's she going to do if she can't even beat a fifty-five-year-old guy with one foot in the grave? What are people going to think of

women's tennis after that? She's going to have a lot of
pressure on her. I love tension. Not that there will be
that much on me. I thrive—I have always played my
best under tension. Whereas just the opposite is true
with her. We're going to be playing in front of the biggest audience ever to see a tennis match, right here at
San Diego Country Estates."

It was difficult to distinguish how much of Riggs's
remarks were put on, how much mere hysteria, and
how much utterly sincere babble, but I finally concluded after hearing the routine some two dozen times
that underneath all that surface male chauvinism was
heartfelt male chauvinism, heightened, in this case, by
Riggs's bitterness toward open tennis.

All the older men tennis players are dismayed that
open tennis, with its huge prize money, came too late
for them to take advantage of it. That women are playing open tennis, too, and in some cities even beginning
to outdraw the men's tour, that a player like Margaret
Court can earn $100,000 a year—this is almost more
than a man like Riggs can bear. Instead of playing in
high-stakes tournaments, Riggs has been forced in the
past twenty-five years to play the kind of tennis he
really prefers, hustling opponents with poodles tied
to his legs, umbrellas and suitcases in hand, top hat on
his head.

Stories of Riggs's hustling have been legendary in
the sports world, and the press managed to dredge
most of them up again for this match. What few in the
press realized, though, was that they were being conned
at least as cleverly as Mrs. Court. Eighteen of the
twenty-four reporters covering the match picked Margaret Court to win, most of them in straight sets. Explanations of sentimentality and sheer stupidity aside,
the reason for all this faulty judgment had mainly to
do with the amazing total performance Riggs put on the
week before the match. Whenever the press watched
him practice, he played well under his game. Whenever he interviewed, he discoursed at length on his fail-

ing strength. He spent days fighting for a lightweight ball, lost in a flip he referred to as "the flip of the century," and spent days sulking about how the weight of the balls would permanently cripple his game. After the match, of course, he confessed he had wanted the heavy-duty balls all along and had just made the fuss to throw Mrs. Court off.

The scene over the weight of the balls was just one of several incidents that served to cloud the already murky male-female issues. Most men would have wanted to flip for heavy-duty balls, while women per- fer lightweight ones; Riggs uses the lighter aluminum racket while Court plays with wood; Riggs's game is all lobs and slices and spins and twists, while Court plays the serve-and-volley technique favored by strong male players. What happened as a result was that the press covering the match, all of whom were male except for me, became far more interested and threat- ened by the women's liberation implications of the rela- tionship between Margaret Court and her husband than by the totally confusing implications of the match itself.

"Look at that," one reporter said to me, pointing to Barry Court, who was carrying the Courts' young son Danny. "He always carries the baby. Margaret never carries the baby." In fact, Mrs. Court carried the baby as often as her husband did when she was off court; this was never registered by the press, who persisted in re- ferring to Barry Court, a tall Australian who manages his wife's career, as "the baby-sitter." Sunday night, af- ter Mrs. Court had been trounced by Riggs, I was walking back to my room and bumped into Brent Musberger of CBS. "Do you know who the real win- ner of today's match was?" he asked. Yes, I thought, I know exactly who the real winner was. Bobby Riggs. That, however, was obviously not the answer Musber- ger was going for. "Who?" I asked. "Barry Court," he replied. "What are you talking about?" I asked. "It's simple," he explained. "Now she'll really need him.

Now she'll really have to depend on him." The notion that Mrs. Court's defeat by a male would somehow alter her relationship with her husband—who has been married to her for six years and presumably came to terms with the bargain at least that long ago—seemed a peculiarly male fantasy. On the other hand, it may be my peculiarly feminist fantasy to believe that Barry Court is happy in his life.

And finally, there was the match. No point in dwelling too long on that. Riggs bounced down to the court in a sky-blue workout suit that looked like a pair of Doctor Dentons; he presented his opponent with a bouquet of twenty-four roses that were arranged exactly like a funeral spray. Margaret Court appeared in a specially designed yellow-and-green tennis dress with the word "Margaret" stitched into its high collar; it was exactly the sort of dress Queen Elizabeth would choose to play tennis in. The match began, and by the time the first three games were over, Riggs was in total control: his lovely lollipop game and his psych-out had Margaret blowing her first serves, failing to rush the net, missing shots she had no business missing. "She's just not bright enough," said the man next to me, who happened to be Pancho Segura. The match ended with Riggs winning 6–2, 6–1. "I played awful," said Mrs. Court afterward. "He hit softer than many of the girls I've been playing. I couldn't get my timing. It was one of the worst matches I've played in a long long time." In the end, Margaret provided a perfect illustration of Radcliffe president Matina Horner's thesis on women fearing success. About the only thing she failed to do was cry.

And we were left with Bobby Riggs. Margaret Court went off to her room—the baby was sick, her husband explained—and Riggs held the press conference alone. Two hours later, when I left San Diego Country Estates, he was still talking. He was planning to enter the Virginia Slims tournament and would even consider wearing a dress. He was knocking women's tennis. He was contemplating a match against Bille Jean King.* "Tell her she has to play for fifty thousand dollars a side," he said. "And she's got to put up the money. I'm not putting up any more free shots. I've done enough for these women." He was describing the last-minute bets he had made and won. He was plugging his vitamin pills and waving his copper bracelet. He was pumping for senior tennis. "The girls say they should get as much money as men," he was saying. "Well, if girls should get as much as men, us seniors should get as much as the girls. Look at this. One of the best woman players beaten by a fifty-five-year-old guy with one foot in the grave." Every so often, you turn a corner and Life, or the times, or the public-relations mechanism that makes the world go round throws out a hero you have to live with for a while.

September, 1973

---

* The Riggs–King match was held in September, 1973. I never wrote anything about it afterward—partly because I didn't want to repeat myself and partly because I had mixed feelings about the outcome. I knew that it was a triumph for women's tennis, and it was even a small triumph for the women journalists at it—we won $800 from Riggs. But when the circus was over, I felt sorry for Riggs. I thought he was a harmless goniff, and I was sad that his fifteen minutes were up—it had been fun.

Dorothy Parker

Eleven years ago, shortly after I came to New York, I met a young man named Victor Navasky. Victor was trying relentlessly at that point to start a small humor magazine called *Monocle,* and there were a lot of meetings. Some of them were business meetings, I suppose; I don't remember them. The ones I do remember were pure social occasions, and most of them took place at the Algonquin Hotel. Every Tuesday at 6 p.m., we would meet for drinks there and sit around pretending to be the Algonquin Round Table. I had it all worked out: Victor got to be Harold Ross, Bud Trillin and C. D. B. Bryan alternated at Benchley, whoever was fattest and grumpiest got to be Alexander Woollcott. I, of course, got to be Dorothy Parker. It was all very heady, and very silly, and very self-conscious. It was also very boring, which disturbed me. Then Dorothy Parker, who was living in Los Angeles, gave a seventieth-birthday interview to the Associated Press, an interview I have always thought of as the beginning of the Revisionist School of Thinking on the Algonquin Round Table, and she said that it, too, had been boring. Which made me feel a whole lot better.

I had never really known Dorothy Parker at all. My parents, who were screenwriters, knew her when I was a child in Hollywood, and they tell me I met her at several parties where I was trotted out in pajamas to meet the guests. I don't remember that, and neither, I suspect, did Dorothy Parker. I met her again briefly when I was twenty. She was paying a call on Oscar

Levant, whose daughter I grew up with. She was frail and tiny and twinkly, and she shook my hand and told me that when I was a child I had had masses of curly black hair. As it happens, it was my sister Hallie who had had masses of curly black hair. So there you are.

None of which is really the point. The point is the legend. I grew up on it and coveted it desperately. All I wanted in this world was to come to New York and be Dorothy Parker. The funny lady. The only lady at the table. The woman who made her living by her wit. Who wrote for *The New Yorker*. Who always got off the perfect line at the perfect moment, who never went home and lay awake wondering what she ought to have said because she had said exactly what she ought to have. I was raised on Dorothy Parker lines. Some were unbearably mean, and some were sad, but I managed to fuzz those over and remember the ones I loved. My mother had a first-rate Parker story I carried around for years. One night, it seems, Dorothy Parker was playing anagrams at our home with a writer named Sam Lauren. Lauren had just made the word "currie," and Dorothy Parker insisted there was no such spelling. A great deal of scrapping ensued. Finally, my mother said she had some curry in the kitchen and went to get it. She returned with a jar of Crosse & Blackwell currie and showed it to Dorothy Parker. "What do they know?" said Parker. "Look at the way they spell Crosse."

I have spent a great deal of my life discovering that my ambitions and fantasies—which I once thought of as totally unique—turn out to be clichés, so it was not a surprise to me to find that there were other young women writers who came to New York with as bad a Dorothy Parker problem as I had. I wonder, though, whether any of that still goes on. Whatever illusions I managed to maintain about the Parker myth were given a good sharp smack several years ago, when John Keats published a biography of her called *You Might As Well Live* (Simon & Schuster). By that time, I had come to grips with the fact that I was not, nor would I ever be, Dorothy Parker; but I had managed to keep myself from what anyone who has read a line about or by her should have known, which was simply that Dorothy Parker had not been terribly good at being Dorothy Parker either. In Keats's book, even the wonderful lines, the salty remarks, the softly murmured throw-aways seem like dreadful little episodes in Leonard Lyons's column. There were the stories of the suicide attempts, squalid hotel rooms, long incoherent drunks, unhappy love affairs, marriage to a homosexual. All the early, sharp self-awareness turned to chilling self-hate. "Boy, did I think I was smart," she said once. "I was just a little Jewish girl trying to be cute."

A year or so after the Keats book, I read Lillian Hellman's marvelous memoir, *An Unfinished Woman* (Little, Brown). In it is a far more affectionate and moving portrait of Parker, one that manages to convey how special it was to be with her when she was at her best. "The wit," writes Hellman, "was never as attractive as the comment, often startling, always sudden, as if a curtain had opened and you had a brief and brilliant glance into what you would never have found for yourself." Still, the Hellman portrait is of a sad lady who misspent her life and her talent.

In one of several unbelievably stupid remarks that do so much to make the Keats biography as unsatisfying as it is, he calls Parker a "tiny, big-eyed feminine woman with the mind of a man." There are only a few things that remain clear to me about Dorothy Parker, and one of them is that the last thing she had was the mind of a man. *The Portable Dorothy Parker* (Viking) contains most of her writing; there are first-rate stories in it—"Big Blonde," of course—and first-rate light verse. But the worst work in it is characterized by an almost unbearably girlish sensibility. The masochist. The victim. The sentimental woman whose moods are totally ruled by the whims of men. This last verse, for example, from "To a Much Too Unfortunate Lady":

He will leave you white with woe
If you go the way you go.
If your dreams were thread to weave,
He will pluck them from his sleeve.
If your heart had come to rest,
He will flick it from his breast.
Tender though the love he bore,
You had loved a little more. . . .
Lady, go and curse your star,
Thus Love is, and thus you are.

What seems all wrong about these lines now is not their emotion—the emotion, sad to say, is dead on—but that they seem so embarrassing. Many of the women poets writing today about love and men write with as much wit as Parker, but with a great deal of healthy anger besides. Like Edna St. Vincent Millay's poetry, which Parker was often accused of imitating, Dorothy Parker's poetry seems dated not so much because it is or isn't but because politics have made the sentiments so unfashionable in literature. The last thing I mean to write here is one of those articles about the woman artist as some sort of victim of a sexist society; it is, however, in Parker's case an easy argument to make.

And so there is the legend, and there is not much of it left. One no longer wants to be the only woman at the table. One does not want to spend nights with a group of people who believe that the smartly chosen rejoinder is what anything is about. One does not even want to be published in *The New Yorker*. But before one looked too hard at it, it was a lovely myth, and I have trouble giving it up. Most of all, I'm sorry it wasn't true. As Dorothy Parker once said, in a line she suggested for her gravestone: "If you can read this, you've come too close."

October, 1973

A Star Is Born

A few months ago, I got a phone call from a man at CBS named Sandy Socolow. I have known Sandy Socolow ever since college, when I was a copy girl at CBS for a summer and he was working for Walter Cronkite. A few years later, he and his wife, Nan, and their children and I all lived in the same New York apartment house, One University Place. As a matter of fact, the night of the 1965 blackout Nan Socolow and I spent a rather ragged evening together. I had groped my way down to her apartment, having nowhere better to go, having no idea that I ought to be doing something memorable that night to tell my children about, and Nan suggested we play canasta. I had forgotten how, but she taught me. She won the first game. I wiped her out in the second. After it, Nan looked up and said, "It's too bad you have to leave." Anyway, I have a fondness for Sandy Socolow in spite of the fact that his wife is a sore loser, and I was glad to hear from him.

"Let's have lunch," he said. "I want to talk to you about your future in television and mine."

"I hate television," I said.

"Let's have lunch anyway," he said.

A few weeks passed between the phone call and the lunch, and during that time I read that CBS was revamping its morning news show and was looking for an anchorwoman and anchorman. I became more interested in the lunch. I really do hate television—last year I did a pilot for a talk show for women, and when it was through, and, as far as I was concerned, perfect, the head of the company that produced the show saw it and said I had a quality on screen not unlike Howard Cosell. The show was cut to pieces, I was fired, and an entire other person was dubbed in my place. All in all, it was not a happy story, and it left me almost certain I never wanted anything serious to do with the medium again. I say *almost* certain, because the only desire I was left with, the only ambition the experience did not manage to kill, was for Barbara Walters's job. I have always wanted Barbara Walters's job. The CBS thing seemed about as close to it as I was ever going to get.

So Sandy Socolow and I had lunch. I told him I had read about the job in the papers. "That's what I was calling you about," he said. It was a nice lunch. Soft-shell crabs. Rice pudding with a lot of raisins in it. I had some ideas. He had some ideas. He said he'd call me after he looked at an old tape of me on *The Dick Cavett Show*. He also said that his wife would be delighted to hear I was separated from my husband, because she had a lot of extra men.

The next day Nan Socolow called.

"Are you free for dinner Tuesday night?" she said.

"Sure," I said.

"Good," she said. "We're having dinner with a man who's a writer, and we'd like you to come, but it's not a fix-up."

"Fine," I said.

"I really want to make that clear," she said. "It's not a fix-up."

"What are you trying to tell me?" I asked. "Is he gay?"

"No," said Nan. "It's not that. It's just that we have to have dinner with him, and we have to have dinner with you, and I thought we'd kill two birds with one stone."

I passed on the dinner.

A few days later—June now—Sandy Socolow's secretary called quite frantically to set up a lunch. He had apparently seen my Cavett tape and was still interested.

I went to the lunch to find Sandy and Lee Townsend, the producer of the show, Gordon Manning, one of the heads of CBS News, and Hughes Rudd, who had just been given the job of anchorman on the new morning show. Part of the purpose of the lunch was to see whether Hughes and I had chemistry. We had chemistry. I have always liked Hughes—he is funny and dry. I like Sandy. I liked Lee Townsend. As for Gordon Manning —when I first came to New York, I ran copy at *Newsweek,* where he was executive editor, and I was forever bearing memos from him that he had written "nifty" across the top of. I am constitutionally incapable of truly relating to anyone whose favorite adjective is nifty. Still, it was a pretty good lunch. Lamb chops. Crème caramel. It was also a seductive lunch, and I left it wanting the job. I also left it knowing that if I got it, it would probably be the worst thing that ever happened to me, the worst hours, the end of my privacy, my private life, my writing. "If you take the job," the man who used to be my husband said to me, "the only person in New York you'll be able to have an affair with is Hughes Rudd." I thought about that, and about the other drawbacks, and I knew that I would never have the courage or good sense to turn it down. It made me crazy.

"What do you want to do?" asked my psychoanalyst in the middle of it all.

"I want them not to offer it to me so I won't have to make a decision," I said.

"That's ridiculous," said my psychoanalyst.

"I'm not sure it is," I said.

It got to be the middle of June. The *Esquire* issue on women, which I had worked on, was on the stands. CBS booked me onto the *Morning News* show, ostensibly to give the magazine a plug but actually to audition me. I got up at 6 a.m., tried not to think about what life would be like if I had to be awake at that hour five days a week, put on my most grown-up dress, and went over to be interviewed by John Hart.

"You did fine," he said after it was over. "I hope you win."

"Who else is up for it?" I asked.

"Well," he said, "the front runner is Sally Quinn."

There is no way, particularly at this point, particularly since the outcome of this contest is no secret, for me to convey the exact pain I felt at that moment. It had something to do with my stomach and something to do with dizziness. For one thing, I knew it was all over, that I would never get the job. For another—and I'll go into this in a minute—it seemed hopelessly ironic.

"Gordon Manning is really hot for her," said John Hart.

"That doesn't surprise me," I said.

There has been altogether too much written about Sally Quinn, here and elsewhere, in recent months; I am sorry to add to it, but a story's a story. Sally Quinn and I were friends. She came to my house a couple of times. I went to her house a couple of times. She helped me out on a story I wrote about Henry Kissinger. I had known Sally two or three years, had seen her over a dozen times, but until the A. J. Liebling Counter-Convention last May, I had never heard her discuss her philosophy of reporting. I never even knew she had one.

As it turned out, she did. She appeared on a panel at the convention, leaned into the microphone, and went on huskily and at some length about being a woman reporter. She said that the essence of reporting was manipulation—through flirtation, the insinuation of availability, a few too many drinks for the interview subject, whatever means were necessary. "Being blond," she said very very slowly, "doesn't hurt." I found all of it incredibly offensive, and said as much to one of Sally's rivals on the Washington *Post,* who quoted me to that effect. Then I spent a few weeks trying to figure out why I had been so upset. At first, it seemed to me it was because I thought what she was saying was demeaning to the profession and to women in it. Then I realized that that wasn't really true, that the profession would somehow survive her remarks. My second thought, and this came during a period of what I like to think of as mental health, was that I had been upset because I thought that Sally's remarks were demeaning to herself. I saw her at a party in June and said as much.

"You don't really work that way," I said, "and when you say that you do, you're just putting yourself down."

"I do work that way," Sally said. "And so do you. We all do."

As it happens, I don't work that way. I have never worked that way. I am uncomfortable flirting, it requires a great deal of energy and ego, and I manage to do it only a couple of times a year, and not with interview subjects.

But the conversation at the party went on, and we got around to the line about being blond. "If what you meant to say by that," I said, "is one of life's cruel truths, which is that it is better to look good than bad in this world, you picked the one way of saying it that was the most self-aggrandizing and least likely to make anyone hear what your point was."

Sally conceded that there might be some truth to that, that she had chosen her words badly, and I went off thinking I had at least made a small point. Later on, I realized I was wrong. I was reading Pauline Kael's review of Norman Mailer's *Marilyn,* and it suddenly hit me that what Sally Quinn had meant to say when she said, "Being blond doesn't hurt," was simply this: being blond doesn't hurt. I also realized later, much much later, what it was that had bothered me so much about her performance that day. When John Hart told me that she was the front runner for the job, I realized that what had gotten to me was that Sally Quinn was right. Her way worked. Mine didn't. Lillian Hellman said it all a good deal better than I could have, in an interview I had with her this summer. We had gotten to talking about women. "Dashiell Hammett used to say I had the meanest jealousy of all," Miss Hellman said. "I had no jealousy of work, no jealousy of money. I was just jealous of women who took advantage of men, because I didn't know how to do it."

Well, you know how it all ended. Sally Quinn got the job. *New York* magazine wrote an article about her. Sally Quinn said the only reason the magazine had published the article, which was not entirely complimentary, was that Clay Felker, the editor, had offered her a job and she had turned it down. "You were going to be a star," Sally said Felker said to her, "and you should have let me make you one." Clay Felker says he never said that to Sally Quinn, but that's not the point. The point is he is capable of saying it. I know, because a few nights after I read in the *New York Times* that Sally had gotten the job—CBS never bothered to tell me—Clay came to my new apartment and looked around. "Oh, Nora," he said. "You shouldn't have to live like this." And he made me an offer.

And I figured, what the hell.

I figured, why not leave *Esquire* magazine.

I figured there are worse things in this world than letting Clay Felker make you a star.

And here I am.

October, 1973

Women in Israel:
The Myth
of Liberation

TEL AVIV—A number of important and unimportant things seem to fly right out the window in a country like Israel in time of war. One of them is partisan politics, which vanished about a month ago and is now making a tentative and slightly unwelcome comeback now that there is a tentative and slightly unwelcome cease-fire. Another is public transportation—the city buses take the troops to war, and most of them are still sitting out in the Sinai Desert waiting to bring them back. A third is room service—or service of any kind, for that matter. "There's a war on" is the all-purpose excuse. It is offered by the El Al steward to explain why no one on the plane except Abba Eban is being served alcoholic beverages, and it is offered by the hotel operator to explain why it has taken her a full ten minutes to answer the telephone.

Yet another casualty of war—at least for the time being—has been the women's movement here. The women's liberation movement in Israel could, without too much trouble, be packed into a small suite in the Dan Hotel. But in spite of its numbers, it has had considerable impact. Publicity has helped, and there has been a great deal of it, much of it sympathetic and provoking. And while the religious laws of Israel, which

148

govern all family and marital matters, are not particularly outrageous in the context of life in the Middle East, there are people here who prefer to think of themselves as part of the Western world, and in that context the laws are extraordinarily backward.

One example of this has become known as the Case of the Mistaken *Mamzerim*. Under religious law, the children of a married woman and a man she is not married to are considered *mamzerim*, or bastards, and they are not allowed to marry Jews who are legitimate —are not, in fact, allowed to marry anyone but other *mamzerim*. (Significantly, this law does not apply to the illegitimate children of married men and single women.) Last year, when there was time to be concerned with such matters, the country spent several months mesmerized by a fascinating case of *mamzerism*. Many years before, a Polish-Jewish woman had eloped with a gentile. They were married and moved to Israel, and he converted to Judaism. Then they were divorced. The woman remarried, this time to a Jew, but she forgot to tell the rabbi who performed the ceremony that she had been divorced. She had children—a son and a daughter. Twenty years later, both children joined the army, and the son went to apply for a marriage certificate. In the course of going through his papers, the rabbinical authorities discovered his mother's failure to mention her divorce. They promptly ruled the second marriage invalid, declared the offspring *mamzerim*, and said that the son could not marry his intended. Not surprisingly, there was a huge public outcry, and the case was appealed to one of the chief rabbis, Shlomo Goren, who is something of a diplomat as chief rabbis go. After holding a hearing, Rabbi Goren managed to find a way to declare the mother's first marriage illegal (and hence, her second marriage legal), on the ground that her first husband, although a convert, had clung to Christian ways. This fact was established conclusively in court when neighbors testified that they had seen him through the bathroom window sitting in the tub drinking vodka and eating pork. The *mamzerim* were pronounced legitimate after all.

Cases of this sort pop up with some frequency, and they have done much to help the women's movement attract attention to the injustice of the religious laws. Before the war began, the movement had attained, if not actual momentum, a fairly constant chugging pace —it had begun to hold demonstrations, file lawsuits against employers, and organize consciousness-raising groups. Now, though, these concerns seem rather trivial against the background of crisis in the Middle East, and members of the two main women's liberation groups in Jerusalem and Tel Aviv seem a bit puzzled as to whether their cause, which had historically done better in times of peace and prosperity, is at all relevant. And the interesting thing is not just that it is in many ways more relevant than ever, but that the war may, quite by accident, bring about substantial improvements for women here.

There is, of course, a prevalent belief in Israel, as well as in the rest of the world, that this country is some sort of paradise for women. To begin with, there is Golda Meir, and her extraordinary achievements are constantly used as an argument against the need for liberation—as in "How can you say women are discriminated against when we have a woman Prime Minister?" In fact, Golda is simply Golda, and she is frequently referred to, in a line that is regarded as a witticism, as "the only man in the Cabinet." What is more to the point is that she is not only the only woman in the Cabinet, but also the only woman who has *ever* served in the Cabinet. Mrs. Meir has never shown any active interest in women's rights—she is a classic example of the successful woman who believes that because she managed to rise to the top, anyone can. Furthermore, her coalition government—like others before it—cooperates with the religious party. The rabbis keep quiet about military spending, and in exchange the politicians keep their hands off the religious laws.

The second factor that contributes to the myth concerns women and the army. Israel is the only country in the world with compulsory military service for women. What is not as well known is that women in the Israeli Army do the clerical and service tasks and leave the important work—which is to say, the fighting and killing—to the men. This was not always true. Before the establishment of the state, women were routinely used as soldiers—first in the Jewish Brigade, next in the underground, and then in the War of Independence. But after 1948, the population increase and religious influence combined to push the women into minor roles—they are not even used as drivers behind the lines, a job frequently given to WACs and the like in supposedly less liberated armies. The women in the Israeli Army today are regarded with exactly the same sort of protective instincts men have always felt toward women in time of war. In the first days of the 1973 war, there was a recurrent rumor here that six women in the Israeli Army had been captured, raped, and killed by the Syrians. The Israelis who repeated it seemed far more outraged by the fate of these women, who turned out not to exist, than by that of the hundreds of men who died fighting in the Golan Heights. It is one of the paradoxes of a male-dominated society that the price of a woman's life is seen to be higher than that of a man's.

The price of her work is not. In 1970, the average yearly income of a woman in communications was 61 percent of a man's—and in just three years this figure has dropped to 42 percent. A woman working in a public service earns 67 percent of a man's salary. Although half the university graduates are women, they are only 2 percent of the full professors in universities, 7 percent of the lawyers, and 5 percent of the engineers. (In contrast, women make up 38 percent of the medical profession.) Women in Israel tend to be employed in jobs that have always been female strongholds—secretarial work and teaching, for example. More important, barely 30 percent of the women between the ages of fifteen and sixty-five work full-time. This, in large part, is due to the widespread prejudice among both Oriental and Western Jews against working women, a prejudice that is reinforced by the rabbis and results in minimal day-care facilities and no legal abortions.

The rabbis oversee all affairs having to do with marriage and divorce—and they do this with 3,000 years of Biblical tradition, much of which would be sheer balderdash if it were not so grotesquely sexist. An Israeli woman is required to go to a *mikvah* before her wedding—and it is estimated that 90 percent of the women married in this unorthodox country comply. The *mikvah* is the ritual bath originally based on primitive beliefs about the uncleanness of female genitalia following the menstrual period; the baths are staffed by older women, some of whom persist in believing that ordinary hygiene will not do the trick and who are notorious for passing on a series of updated superstitions about what they call "the dirty days." One particularly common example of this nowadays is the belief that a woman who touches her husband during her period will cause him to be killed in the next war. A woman who does not want to go to a *mikvah* has two choices: she can bribe someone to sign a paper saying she had been to one, or she can go to Cyprus to be married by a justice of the peace. This practice has become so commonplace of late that the leader of Cyprus is often referred to as Rabbi Makarios.

"According to civil law, women are equal to men," says Shulamit Aloni, the lawyer and politician who is the leading spokeswoman for women's rights here. "But I have to go to a religious court as far as personal affairs are concerned. Only men are allowed to be judges there—men who pray every morning to thank

God He did not make them women. You meet prejudice before you open your mouth. And because they believe women belong in the home, you are doubly discriminated against if you work."

No woman may testify in a religious court: hence, no woman may be divorced without her husband's consent. Several years ago, a woman whose husband had been jailed for child-molesting asked for a divorce; he refused, and there the matter rested. A woman without children who is widowed may not remarry without the consent of her husband's unmarried brother or, failing that, a formal exemption from the rabbinical court. Some three hundred cases have been disputed under this law since the 1967 war, and there will be hundreds more as a result of this last conflict. But the most oppressive of the religious laws—and the one most relevant to the current political situation—is the law of *agunot,* which holds that a deserted wife may not remarry under any circumstance. Under Jewish religious law, this prohibition is absolute. What this means is that a woman whose husband is believed dead but whose body has not been recovered may never ever remarry. (However, from time to time, a woman who appeals is sometimes given permission to become a widow.)

Cases arising under the law of *agunot* are often incredibly complicated. After World War II, a Jewish woman who had been in the concentration camps with her husband emigrated to Israel. She believed that her husband had been killed in the camps, and after seven years he was declared dead under an exception to the law of *agunot.* She remarried and had children; thirteen years later, her first husband arrived in Israel, and the children of the second marriage were ruled to be *mamzerim.*

This law accounts in large part for the unusual concern and energy the Israeli Army brings to the often dangerous task of recovering the bodies of its soldiers. Until two years ago, when an Israeli submarine carrying over seventy men sank without a trace, no blanket deviation from this law was ever tolerated. But Rabbi Goren, obviously caught up in his role as a demi-Solomon, went into action and managed to provide a true measure of relief by ruling that the wives of the missing could remarry. The good rabbi will undoubtedly be forced to do something of the sort again: at this point, the discrepancy between Israeli and Arab estimates of the number of prisoners of war held by the Arabs is so vast that it is altogether possible that some four hundred Israeli soldiers' bodies may never be recovered. This will result in some four hundred not-quite-widows, and that is too many not-quite-widows for the law of *agunot* to stand up to. None of the women in Israel in or out of the movement want to go through a war to weaken an oppressive law; in a coalition government of this sort, however, that seems to be the only way.

Another and more far-reaching irony that may result from this war is that the status of women in the work force may improve substantially. The general election, which is now scheduled for December 31, is expected to produce at least a slight shift in favor of the right-wing, or more hawkish, political parties—and this in turn may lead to a situation where far more Israeli men are kept mobilized. Whether or not this occurs, a large number of men will be kept at the front simply to hold the cease-fire lines on the West Bank: in the short run, at least, the Israeli government will probably find it necessary to lure some women out of the home and into the factories. (The Israeli G.N.P. is off 40 percent since the beginning of the war.) If more women are needed in the labor force, the government will have to do something about day care for the middle-income women. There is even some talk now about the possibility of setting up a special reserve force for women —not to fight in the army, but to take their husbands' places in the economy during war.

"One of the reasons women's lib isn't catching on as

much as it should," said Ruth Rasnic, a translator who is a member of the Tel Aviv women's liberation group, "is because of this great military myth we have here. The myth is essential—only I think women should take a much more active part in it. Whether women want to work in peacetime is up to them, but they should be made to take part in the economy during a war, because war is inevitable."

And so war and an increased mobilization—which Israeli women do not want—may lead to a situation that improves the status of women here. It is the kind of twist of logic that seems entirely fitting in a country whose citizens take so much delight in calculating every possible consequence of every situation. Besides, like everything else that has flown out the window of late, logic has been in short supply, and for the moment, at least, all is confusion.

November, 1973

The Littlest Nixon

She comes down the aisle, and the clothes are just right, Kimberly-knitted to the knee, and she walks in step with the government official, who happens to be H.E.W. Secretary Caspar Weinberger, and her face is perfect, not smiling mind you—this is too serious an event for that—but bright, intent, as if she is absolutely fascinated by what he is saying. Perhaps she actually is. They take their places on the platform of the Right to Read Conference at Washington's Shoreham Hotel, and he speaks and she speaks and the director of Right to Read speaks. Throughout she listens raptly, smiles on cue, laughs a split second after the audience laughs. Perhaps she is actually amused. On the way out, she says she hopes she will be able to obtain a copy of the speech she has just sat through. Perhaps she actually thought it was interesting. There is no way to know. No way to break through. She has it all down perfectly. She was raised for this, raised to cut ribbons, and now that it has all gone sour, it turns out that she has been raised to deal with that, too.

The Washington press corps thinks that Julie Nixon Eisenhower is the only member of the Nixon Administration who has any credibility—and as one journalist put it, this is not to say that anyone believes what she is saying but simply that people believe *she* believes what she is saying. They will tell you that she is approachable, which is true, and that she is open, which is not. Primarily they find her moving. "There is some-

156

thing about a spirited and charming daughter speaking up for her father in his darkest hour that is irresistibly appealing to all but the most cynical." That from the *Daily News*. And this from NBC's Barbara Walters, signing off after Julie's last appearance on the *Today* show: "I think that no matter how people feel about your father, they're always very impressed to see a daughter defend her father that way."

There *is* something very moving about Julie Nixon Eisenhower—but it is not Julie Nixon Eisenhower. It is the *idea* of Julie Nixon Eisenhower, essence of daughter, a better daughter than any of us will ever be; it is almost as if she is the only woman in America over the age of twenty who still thinks her father is exactly what she thought he was when she was six. This idea is apparently so overwhelming in its appeal that some Washington reporters go so far as to say that Julie doesn't seem like a Nixon at all—a remark so patently absurd as to make one conclude either that they haven't heard a word she is saying or that they have been around Nixon so long they don't recognize a chocolate-covered spider when they see one.

I should point out before going any further that I have a special interest in Presidents' daughters, having spent a good thirty minutes in my youth wanting to be Margaret Truman. And even back then, I knew it was not a perfect existence—Secret Service men trailing you everywhere, life in a fishbowl, and so forth. Still, whatever the drawbacks, it seemed clear that if you were the President's daughter, you at least got to date a lot. The other attraction to the fantasy, I suppose, had to do with the fact that the role of the President's daughter is the closest thing there is in America to being a princess, the closest thing to having stature and privilege purely as a result of an accident of birth. It is one of life's little jokes that both America and Britain have suffered through remarkably similar princesses in recent years: the Johnson girls, the Nixon girls, and Princess Anne are all drab, dull young women who have managed to acquire enough poise and good grooming to get through the public events their parents do not have time to attend.

Julie and Tricia were born just as their father was beginning public life. They grew up in Washington as congressman's daughters, senator's daughters, and Vice-President's daughters. Then they moved to California to be gubernatorial candidate's daughters, and later to New York to be Presidential contender's daughters. After graduating from the Chapin School, Tricia went on to Finch College, Julie to Smith. There she began dating, and married—not a commoner, but a President's grandson. (David Eisenhower, with his endless tables of batting averages and illogical articles on the American left, is the perfect Nixon son-in-law. Still, he is not stupid. Last summer, after working as a sportswriter for the Philadelphia *Bulletin,* he was asked if he had any observations on the American press. "Yes," he reportedly said. "Journalists aren't nearly as interesting as they think they are.")

Marriage—which might logically have been expected to move Julie into a more removed and private existence—has instead strengthened and intensified her family connections and political role. During college, the Eisenhowers spent their summer vacations in a third-floor suite at the White House and took time off from school to campaign for Nixon's re-election. These days, they see Julie's parents several times a week; the Nixons often sneak off to eat with Julie and David in the $125,000 two-bedroom Bethesda home that Bebe Rebozo bought and rented to the Eisenhowers, presumably at well below its market price.

A few months ago, Julie took a full-time job at $10,000 a year at Curtis Publishing, where she is assistant editorial director of children's magazines and assistant editor of the *Saturday Evening Post.* She announced at the time that the children's magazine field attracted her because it would be impossible for her, as the President's daughter, to write for adult magazines on sensitive political subjects. An upcoming article for the *Saturday Evening Post,* however, while hardly on anything sensitive or political, is nonetheless on a topic that could not be more calculated to draw attention to her position: it is a profile of Alice Roosevelt Longworth, who is now eighty-nine and in the seventy-third year of her career as a President's daughter.

Julie, of course, is nothing like Alice Roosevelt, or any of the other flibbertigibbet Presidents' daughters in the history of this country. In the months since the Watergate hearings began, she has become her father's principal defender, his First Lady in practice if not in fact. "It was something I took on myself," she said. "I just thought I had a story to tell, that there were certain points I could make, and I was very eager to do it. The idea that my father has to hide behind anyone's skirts is of course ludicrous." In any case, Julie's skirts were the only ones available: Pat Nixon is uncomfortable in press and television interviews, and Tricia is in New York. (Washington rumor has it that her husband, Edward Cox, and the President do not get on.) "And that leaves me," said Julie.

It has left her to make two appearances on the *Today* show, a television hookup with the BBC, a guest shot on Jack Paar's show. She has survived Kandy Stroud of *Women's Wear Daily* and lunch with Helen Thomas of the U.P.I. and Fran Lewine of the A.P. Odd little personal details about the President have slipped out during these interviews—whether deliberately or not. She has said that her father sometimes doesn't feel like getting up in the morning, that he took the role of devil's advocate in a family discussion on whether he should resign, that he often sits alone at night upstairs in the White House playing the piano. During her last appearance with Barbara Walters, whose interviews with her have been dazzling, she even came up with a sinister-influence theory of her own to explain everything: "Sometimes I think we were born under an unlucky star."

Her performances are always calm and professional and poised, her revelations just titillating enough, and after all, she's only a girl—and the combination of these has tended to draw attention away from the substantive things she is saying and the way she is saying them. Julie Eisenhower has developed—or been coached in—three basic approaches to answering questions. The first is not to answer the question at all. During her BBC appearance, an American woman living in England phoned in to say, "I would like Mrs. Eisenhower to know that her father's actions have made our position abroad untenable . . . it would be better if he came forward and answered questions himself instead of putting you in his place." Julie replied, "I'd like to ask . . . how she thinks my father can answer more on Watergate without pointing the finger at people who have not been indicted." This answer—in addition to skirting the question and making Nixon look like a man whose sole thought is of the Constitution—utterly overlooks the fact that almost everyone connected with Watergate has been called to testify, a good many have been indicted, and some have even been convicted.

The second approach is to point to the bright side. Thus, when she is asked about Watergate, she talks instead of her father's successes with China, Russia, and the Middle East crisis. When she is asked about the number of Presidential appointees who have been forced to resign, she mentions Henry Kissinger and Ron Ziegler, whom she once called "a man of great integrity." "And I'd go beyond that," she said once. "I'd say that many of these people we're talking about, these aides, were great Americans, really devoted to their country, and they didn't make any money on Watergate, they didn't do anything for personal gain.

They made mistakes, errors in judgment. I don't think they're evil men."

The third, and most classic, of Mrs. Eisenhower's techniques is simply to put the blame elsewhere—on the press. She combines the Middle American why-doesn't-the-press-ever-print-good-news theme with good old-fashioned Nixon paranoia. I spoke with her the other day for five minutes, and she spent most of that time complaining that her mother had met the day before with a group from the Conference on the Role of Women in the Economy, and not one word about it had been printed in the papers. "Instead we get all these negative things," she said. When she was asked recently what she thought of Barry Goldwater's charge that her father's credibility was at an all-time low, she replied: "Barry Goldwater also had a press conference during this whole period . . , and he said that the press were hounds of destruction. I don't think he meant all of the press, but, um, Goldwater *is* a quotable man, isn't he? I didn't hear *that* on the networks. But when he says [my father's] credibility is at an all-time low, that *is* on the networks."

The only questions that stump Julie Eisenhower at all are the ones that concern her father's personality. She has said that she is sick of telling reporters what a warm, human person he is—a fact that fortunately has not stopped reporters from pressing her to give examples. One story she produced recently to show what a card her father can be in his off moments concerned the time her husband, David, took the wheel of Bebe Rebozo's yacht—and the President, in response, appeared on deck wearing not one but two life preservers. "He is quite a practical joker," she said on another occasion. "He likes to tease and he likes to plan surprises when he can. Things like getting birthday candles for a cake that don't blow out. You know, all nice and lit and you sit there huffing and puffing and they don't go out. . . . Things like that."

There is no point in dwelling too heavily on the implications of a daughter who has managed to play a larger role in her father's life than his wife seems to. And there is also no point in wondering what is going to happen to Julie Eisenhower's view of her father if the fall actually comes. It is safe to say that breeding will out, and all the years of growing up in that family will protect her from any insight at all, will lead her to conclude that he was quite simply done in by malicious, unpatriotic forces. What is clear, though, is that Julie Nixon Eisenhower is fighting for herself and her position as hard as she is fighting for her father and his. She once said that if her father was forced out of office, she would "just fold up and wither and fall away." What is more likely is that she will deal with that, too, vanish for a couple of years, and then crop up in politics again. That, after all, is what Nixons do, and that, in the end, is all she is.

December, 1973

Divorce,
Maryland Style

The *Ladies' Home Journal* is after her. *Cosmopolitan* is after her. I am after her. All of us think that there is something to the story of Barbara Mandel, something positively paradigmatic. After all, what happened to Barbara Mandel last year happens to thousands of American woman. After thirty-two years of marriage, her husband left her for another woman. Moved into a hotel. Called a lawyer. It happens every day. The difference, in this case, was that Barbara Mandel's husband was Marvin Mandel, the governor of the state of Maryland. And Barbara Mandel was having none of it.

It is safe to say that there was no way Marvin Mandel could have left his wife that would have made her happy; nonetheless, he managed to leave her in a way that was bound to humiliate her as completely as possible. To begin with, he did not even tell her himself. Well, that's not entirely fair: for two years he had been telling her he wanted a divorce, and for two years she had been telling him she would never give him one. But he never told her he was actually moving out; the morning he did, July 3, 1973, he arranged an appointment for her with the family doctor and had him break the news. His press secretary read her the statement over the telephone. And when Barbara Mandel called her husband to beg him to hold off, he informed her that it was too late; the press had already been given the statement.

"I would like to announce that I am separated from Mrs. Mandel," it read. "My decision and separation are final and irrevocable, and I will take immediate action to dissolve the marriage. . . . I am in love with another woman, Mrs. Jeanne Dorsey, and I intend to marry her. Mrs. Mandel and I have had numerous discussions about this matter and she is completely aware of my feelings, of my actions, and of my intentions. . . . Mrs. Mandel and I no longer share mutual interests nor are our lives mutually fulfilling. . . ."

There was not a mention of the good years, the old times spent growing up as childhood sweethearts in northwest Baltimore. There was not a mention of what she had done for him, all those hands she shook, all those ward heelers' names she memorized, all those rooms in the governor's mansion she repainted. He was leaving her. He was leaving her publicly. He was stripping her of her only weapon—the threat of exposing his liaison—by announcing it himself. Barbara Mandel, First Lady of Maryland—that was how she signed the souvenir ashtrays and the 8″ x 10″ glossies —reacted by refusing to go.

"The governor crawled out of my bed this morning," she told the reporters she telephoned that afternoon. "He has never slept anyplace but with me. I think the strain of the job has gotten to him. I'm surprised. Marvin has not discussed this with me. I don't know what in the world he's talking about. I hope the governor will come to his senses on this. You don't take thirty-two years of married life and throw them down the drain." Mrs. Mandel added that she thought her husband "should see a psychiatrist." In the meantime, she said, she would wait for him in the mansion.

So far, a fairly ordinary American tragedy. A woman invests her life in her husband's career, and he pays her back by leaving her. A woman grows up in a society where the only option seems to be to dedicate herself to her husband. "My case is just different because I helped to make him governor," Mrs. Mandel said.

But, of course, that was a big difference—and that is where the case departs abruptly from the paradigm. Barbara Mandel responded to her husband's rejection not just as a wounded wife but as a seasoned politician. She carefully leaked tidbits of information to selected reporters. She allowed one reporter to negotiate on her behalf with the governor's chief aide. Her statement on July 3—which seems on the surface quite hysterical —carefully left the governor a face-saving way to return: he could simply admit that she was right, the pressures of the job *had* gotten to him; now he had come to his senses. Hell hath no fury, it is true; at the same time, it was clear that part of Mrs. Mandel's fury came not just from the fact that there was another woman involved, but also from the suspicion that the other woman wanted to use her husband and his position exactly as much as Mrs. Mandel did.

Marvin Mandel was a young Baltimore lawyer in 1952 when he first entered the state legislature. He was diligent and hard-working; in addition, he was thoroughly introverted. His outgoing wife—who was known as Bootsie, a nickname that she inexplicably rhymes with "footsie"—campaigned and went everywhere with him; she provided the warmth and earthiness he was chronically unable to convey. Mandel rose to become speaker of the House of Delegates. In 1969, after Spiro Agnew left the governorship to become Vice-President, the Mandels moved into the fifty-three-room Georgian governor's mansion in Annapolis. By this time, the governor's relationship with Mrs. Dorsey had been common knowledge around the State House for years; one of Mrs. Dorsey's four children recently told the Washington *Post* that his mother had been seeing Mandel since 1960. Mrs. Dorsey, now thirty-six, was divorced a few years ago from another Maryland legislator; she is a Democrat who served as police commissioner during a stint on her town board. ("I'm not a big story," she told the *Post*'s Judy Bachrach recently, "and there's no reason why I should open my private life to you. Now, frankly, there is a big story and it's right here in Leonardtown. We have this terrific sewage problem.")

Bootsie Mandel was never in the tradition of great first ladies—but compared with her predecessor, she did an energetic, creditable job, and she became more involved in it as her isolation from the governor increased. "God damn it, I'm nothing around here," she told one of her husband's supporters early in his first term. "Before he was governor, I used to drive him everywhere. Now he has a state trooper. I used to help him with his speeches. Now he has a speechwriter. What good am I?" What good she did had mainly to do with the mansion. She refurbished it, printed up lavish programs describing its interior, appeared at charity luncheons to announce that twice-a-week tours through it were available.

At the same time, she had a habit of getting everything she did slightly wrong. At one point, she discovered that a portrait hanging in the mansion had a label attributing it to Hogarth; she promptly insured it for $300,000, scheduled a ceremony and surprise announcement, and was informed by a prominent art historian that the painting wasn't a Hogarth at all. Several years ago, she confounded the entire state legislature by inviting the wives to the annual party celebrating the legislature's adjournment; the party had traditionally been an event for the politicians to be with whatever women they had been seeing on the sly during the session. Said one Baltimore assemblyman: "You cannot overestimate the panic that went through this place that day."

Governor Mandel's relationship with Mrs. Dorsey became increasingly open. In December, 1970, his unmarked state police car hit another car in Prince Georges County and the driver of the other car was

killed. The governor refused to say what he was doing
in an unmarked car after midnight; then he said he
had been at a secret political meeting. Reporters
checked and could not find any other politicians who
had been to a meeting with the governor that night.
When they asked whether he hadn't in fact been re-
turning from St. Marys County, where Mrs. Dorsey
lived, he declined comment. At about that time, Mrs.
Mandel apparently found out that the situation was
serious and began to pump friends for information.
Sometimes she asked straight out; more often, she attempted an approach she seemed to believe was de-
vious. "What do you think the Jewish community would
say about a governor who left his wife for another
woman?" she asked the wife of one of her husband's as-
sociates.

Within a few weeks of the governor's walkout, Mrs.
Mandel realized she had made a terrible mistake. She
had counted on her friends to side with her—and they
sided with the governor and his power. She had counted
on major political repercussions—but there was only
a brief flurry of mail support from middle-aged wom-
en. She had counted on seeming to be a force for
morality—and instead she became an object of ridicule.
"She was playing cards in a game that had ended,"
said one Maryland politician. "It had ended in American politics, in American life, even ended in her narrow circle. Divorce just doesn't mean that much
anymore."

Bootsie carried on. She alerted the press as to her
comings and goings. She appeared at a Washington
literary party and identified herself as the woman who
had knocked Elizabeth Taylor and Richard Burton's
breakup off the front page. She spoke to a group of
Democratic women, many of whom cried as she vowed
to continue as first lady. "I want you to know that I am
a very proud woman," she said, "very very proud of
everything I've done since I've been a little girl. Life
does not always work out the way you want it. . . ."

In the end, what kept Barbara Mandel in the governor's mansion as long as she stayed was not the pathetic hope that her husband would return—she had long given up on that—but the fact that her presence there was the only wedge she had to negotiate a substantial money settlement. Mandel's first offer to his wife, she told friends, was $6,250 a year, a quarter of his yearly salary as governor. Her lawyer ultimately negotiated a six-figure settlement. And on December 20, with a crowd of reporters standing outside the wrought-iron gates, Barbara Mandel moved out, with her hope chest, love seat, artificial flower centerpieces, and eight wardrobe boxes of clothing. "Five and a half months have passed and our marriage has not returned to normal," she said. "Therefore, with deep regret, I am leaving the mansion."

She moved to a two-bedroom apartment in Baltimore—in the same complex where her married son and daughter live—and when I reached her on the telephone, she told me she preferred not to say anything. "I'm very busy," she said. Doing what? I asked. "Just the normal things," she said, "the normal things you have to do for yourself."

"I'll tell you a story," one of her friends said a few days ago. "The day after Marvin moved out, last July, Bootsie went to the family cemetery. She sat looking at the graves, and she wished that he were dead. She felt she would have been better off as a widow. I can't help thinking she was right."

January, 1974

Rose Mary Woods— The Lady or the Tiger?

It all depends on whom you talk to. Everything does, as it happens, but the case of Rose Mary Woods depends so much on whom you talk to that the more people you talk to, the more confused everything becomes. People in Washington talk to each other about Rose Mary Woods a great deal these days, and the conversations always end up sounding like the third-to-last chapter in an Agatha Christie mystery. Loose ends. Nothing but loose ends. The Uher tape recorder. The mysteriously elliptical testimony of J. Fred Buzhardt. The White House allegation that the subpoena did not cover the Haldeman conversation. The weekend at Camp David. The weekend in Key Biscayne. The role of Stephen Bull. And at the center of it all is Rose Mary. Dear, sweet, considerate, thoughtful, devout, loyal, put-upon Rose Mary. Tough, cunning, crafty, complicated, powerful, fanatical Rose Mary. Which one is Rose Mary: the lady or the tiger? It all depends on whom you talk to.

"Everybody on God's earth is against her," Charles Rhyne is saying. "The power of the judiciary, the White House lawyers, the prosecutors, the tape experts. There's never been a setup like this one. How can she stand up against all this by herself? She's got the grand

169

jury, the Common Cause people, the milk people, the Watergate committee—all of them are after her." Charles Rhyne is Rose Mary Woods's lawyer, has been since the day after Thanksgiving, two days after Miss Woods, who has been Richard Nixon's personal secretary some twenty-three years, was told she had better go out and find a lawyer of her own, because the White House lawyers would not represent her on this one. The problem, of course, had to do with an eighteen-and-a-half-minute gap on a White House tape made June 20, 1972, three days after the Watergate break-in. And the reason the White House lawyers cast Rose Mary Woods out to pay her own legal fees was that they thought she might well be responsible for every buzzing second of it. Charles Rhyne is outraged by the whole business. He is a former president of the American Bar Association, the lawyer Central Casting sends out when you ask for Integrity, a man of impeccable connections (most of whom he appears with in photographs on his office wall), a classmate and good friend of Richard Nixon's from Duke Law School, and his North Carolina-accented voice becomes positively mellifluous as he assures the press that his client was sold down the river. To prove it, he pulls out a transcript of a conference held the day before Thanksgiving, November 21, 1973, when White House counsels J. Fred Buzhardt and Leonard Garment finally went to Judge John J. Sirica to tell him they had discovered a gap on the tape.

"Judge, we have a problem," Buzhardt began that day. "In the process of preparing the analysis . . . one of the tapes, the intelligence is not available for approximately eighteen minutes. You can't hear the voices. . . . Under the circumstances, we know at this point that it looks quite serious. It doesn't appear from what we know at this point that it could be accidental."

"Does not appear?" Sirica asked.

"Does not appear from the information we have at this point," Buzhardt said. "At its worst, it looks like a very serious thing, Your Honor. If there is an explanation, quite frankly, I don't know what it is at the moment. . . ."

"Who was the last one that actually listened to this particular tape?" Sirica asked.

"The original? The original, according to the record, was first checked out to Miss Woods."

"Was it all right before it was checked out to Miss Woods?" Sirica asked.

"We don't know . . ." Buzhardt said. "I guess she is the only one [who] listened to it. . . . Then the circumstance is even a little worse than that, Your Honor."

"I don't know if it could get much worse," said Sirica.

"Just wait," said Leonard Garment.

"As you know, Your Honor," Buzhardt went on, "the notes were subpoenaed, too. We found Mr. Haldeman's notes on this meeting. . . . The notes reflect that the discussion was about Watergate. . . . When you get past the Watergate typed notes . . . that is where the tape picks up. . . . Maybe I am out of line for saying this, but quite frankly I think Miss Woods ought to have time to reflect on this and she ought to have time to secure counsel."

The meeting ended with Sirica's scheduling a hearing for the following Monday, November 26. Leonard Garment accepted a subpoena for Rose Mary Woods to appear there—and telephoned her to say he was doing so. He returned to the White House and sent it over to her with a note. "Here is the subpoena we discussed earlier," it read. "Love, Len."

" 'Love, Len,' " Charles Rhyne says, shaking his head. "Her own lawyers plead her guilty, then say she ought to get counsel of her own, then accept a subpoena for her when they've admitted they aren't her lawyers any longer, and then send it over and sign it with love. Of course, I didn't know anything about this in the beginning. The day after that meeting, on Thanksgiving Day, I was called by General Haig and he asked me to come down. He told me that Rose had been told to get a lawyer and was very upset. I've known Rose twenty-three years. I called her and told her to calm down, that I'd come down the next morning.

"So on Friday I go down and speak to Haig and he sends me over to see Garment and Buzhardt. 'She did it,' they said to me. 'No question about it. We ran tests on the lamp and the typewriter. So sorry. We don't know what you can do for her.' I went over to see Rose. She was enormously upset. I've never seen Rose upset. She said she didn't know what was going on. 'For the last week,' she said, 'everyone's been treating me like a leper.' 'Well, Rose,' I said, 'I've talked to Garment and Buzhardt and they say you knocked eighteen and a half minutes off this tape.' She just blew up. She said she'd known me a long long time and she was going to tell me everything. She would not accept responsibility for that. She hadn't done it. She wouldn't say she'd done it. She would not let them say she'd done it. She told me about the accident she had had October first with the tape, that she might have knocked four minutes off it. 'But,' she said, 'what really haunts me is that I never heard a word on that part of the tape.' I talked to her for three or four hours. I listened to the tape. And I said to her, 'I believe you.'

"This poor secretary, without any government money, all alone," said Rhyne. "I stand between her and the world."

Aunt Rose. That is what Tricia and Julie call her. She is family. Dick and Pat and Tricia and Julie and David and Bebe and Rose. She baby-sat for the girls. She exchanged clothes with Pat. Her brother Joe, a former F.B.I. man who served as sheriff of Cook County, used to wear Richard Nixon's hand-me-down suits. She attends family dinners in the White House. The President relaxes with her. He kids her—and it is not even labored. He becomes openly irritated with her—and he does that only with people he is close to. She is the person his own relatives call when they want to get through to him: the night of the first debate against Kennedy in the 1960 election, Nixon's mother, Hannah, called Rose Woods—not Pat Nixon—to say she thought her son looked a bit under the weather. Rose has been through it all. She took dictation for the telegram he wanted sent to General Eisenhower withdrawing from the 1952 ticket after the slush-fund charges— and she would have torn it up herself but for the fact that Murray Chotiner did it instead. She was in the car when they were stoned in Caracas, in the kitchen in Moscow; she followed him to Los Angeles and New York during the long out-of-office stretch. "I was his, I suppose you could say, personal secretary, aide, wastebasket emptier, anything else," she testified recently. "I was the only person who worked for him at that time."

"When I heard about it," said a man who used to work in the White House, "when I heard that Rose Woods had to go out and get a lawyer, I thought, Well, that's it. They have now reached the point where they're having hand-to-hand combat in the Oval Office."

The relationship between Rose Mary Woods and Richard Nixon is a complicated one. He counts on her. He respects her judgment on political matters, particularly where people are concerned. She is not afraid to disagree with him, even to snap back at him. In *Six Crises,* Nixon calls her "one of my most honest critics," and says, "She has that rare and unique characteristic that marks the difference between a good secretary and a great one—she is always at her best when the pressures are greatest." The emotional content of their relationship fascinates people.

"She's a little like the choir member in the Baptist church who falls in love with the minister," says one administration insider. "It's the classic Christian fantasy of the virgin and God—and obviously a part of the fantasy is that nothing ever happens. It just remains a kind of worship."

"Have you ever been in love?" asks another man who considers himself a friend to both Nixon and Miss Woods. "Really in love? Over a long period of time? She's been in love with Nixon—though not at all in a sexual sense—for over twenty years. Have you ever played poker? She's an extremely good poker player in the political world. She's smart, tough, ruthless, experienced, all the things you have to be. And she plays on behalf of Nixon, not on behalf of herself.

"Rose has provided him with the feeling that there was support for him and his cause, emotional sustenance at times when there really wasn't anyone else —not even Pat. At various times, Pat laid down the law and said, 'No more politics.' Rose always encouraged him to persevere. Another thing she does is to provide him with emotional and intellectual justification. During the period prior to the 1968 convention, she was always ready with criticisms of his rivals. In the fall of 1967, Lyn Nofziger, Reagan's press agent, broke the story of the homosexual ring that was active at the top level of Reagan's administration. Rose had found out about it a few weeks before, and I remember a dinner with her and Nixon where she presented that to us, saying, in effect, that that was what one could expect from Reagan, that he would be so careless about his staff selection he couldn't possibly be a good President."

There has always been a slight tinge of the martyr in the way Miss Woods operated with Nixon. In early 1969, when she was engaged in a power struggle with H. R. Haldeman and became so disturbed by it that she considered leaving her job, she never once mentioned what was going on to the President. And according to Charles Rhyne, the President has never once referred to, much less reassured his secretary about, her legal problems since the gap was found on November 14, when she claims she told him that she might well be responsible for four or five minutes of it, but would not take the blame for the full eighteen. Rose Woods presumably would never think to bring the question up herself. The only family or administration member who has spoken up for Rose since then has been Julie Nixon Eisenhower, who called her "a woman of complete integrity. She would never commit a criminal act."

Rose Mary Woods went to work for Nixon on February 21, 1951, just after he had been elected to the Senate. She is red-headed, well groomed, with a peaches-and-cream complexion. She gives the impression of being quite petite, and her friends say that she is somewhat frail physically and has suffered periodic bouts of pneumonia from overwork. She has literally worked seven-day, hundred-hour weeks, fifty-two weeks a year for twenty-three years—and in many ways she is not at all unique. There are thousands of women like her in Washington, women who come here as girls, get secretarial jobs on Capitol Hill, devote their lives to politicians, and end up elderly spinsters, living on their government pensions in apartments full of political knickknacks.

"They are a special twentieth-century breed," Helen Dudar wrote in the New York *Post,* "those ladies who guard the boss's door and fend off the telephone calls and read his mail; women largely without private lives because the real world is right there in the vortex spinning around the great man; women usually without husbands because the job takes most of their time and energies; women with small fiefdoms of their own encompassing sub-secretaries, the Xerox machine, the messenger service, and some nervous stenographers. Selfless, happily job-enslaved, eager to be useful, they are the vestal virgins in the temples of business and politics, the Indispensables, the private secretaries."

"It's a very exciting life," said Doris Jones, secretary to former Nixon aide Robert Finch and a close friend of Miss Woods's. "You get caught up in it. You get so busy. The next thing you know, you turn around and your're forty-five or fifty years old and unmarried, and you hadn't intended for it to work out that way at all. I know I never did."

Rose Mary Woods came to Washington from Sebring, Ohio, where she was born fifty-five years ago, the middle child of five children. Her parents were devout Catholics; her father worked at the Royal China Company, first as a potter, then as foreman, finally as personnel director. Her parents died a few years ago, and Miss Woods refers to them frequently: her father, she says, was a temperamental Irishman, while her mother was a calm, pacific woman. "Rose is a strange combination of Irish fire and quiet determination," says Robert Gray, a public-relations executive at Hill & Knowlton, who is Miss Woods's most frequent escort. "She often says, 'I've got to pray to God to let my mother's cool head prevail, and not my father's temper.' "

But for a series of misfortunes, Rose Mary Woods would probably have grown up to lead a traditional small-town Midwestern life. But in her last year at McKinley High School, she contracted a mysterious disease. "I weighed eighty-two pounds," she once said. "It was a growth. It may well have been cancer. Nobody knows. They X-rayed it and it disappeared. I wasn't able to work when I first got out. I wasn't able to go to school." Ultimately, she recovered and went to work as a secretary at Royal China; she became engaged to a young man who died. In 1943, she came to Washington. "I had a sister here who had a very tragic personal problem and I was the only one who could come." The sister was employed at the Office of Censorship, and Miss Woods went to work there, too. After the war, she joined the International Training Administration and then a committee on Capitol Hill run by Christian Herter. There she came to the attention of Richard Nixon, then a young congressman, and he to hers. She has often said that she was very much impressed by him before she even knew him, because he kept such neat expense accounts.

In the 1950s, Miss Woods lived on California Street in Washington, first in an apartment she shared with an elderly woman, then in a studio apartment of her own. She had almost no time for the few activities she favors—dancing, duckpin bowling, entertaining—and her moments of leisure were mostly spent grabbing sandwiches with other Capitol Hill secretaries. These women—who are still close to her—paint a picture of Rose Mary Woods and her life that is low-key and muted. They emphasized her devout Catholicism, her sacrifices, the thoughtful favors she does for friends, her total integrity. They believe every word she has testified, assure you she would never have done anything like what she has been accused of. "She'd probably lay down her life for Richard Nixon," says her friend Winnie De Weese, who used to be with the Republican Policy Committee, "but she would never lie for him."

Another close friend, Eloise De La O, former secretary to Senator Clinton Anderson, says, "I called her the night I heard she had gotten a lawyer. She said to me, 'You know, Eloise, my boss would never ask me to do anything like that.' She is a good Christian, a good Catholic, a practicing Catholic. You don't do things like that if that's the kind of person you are. Somebody is trying to do something to her."

The men who have known Rose Woods over the years tell a slightly different story. "There was a story about her dancing the tango alone one night at San Clemente," said one man. "Don't let it confuse you. Don't make the mistake of thinking of her as a sad, fragile, overworked secretary. She's a complicated woman who's been at the center for twenty-five years." And the men tend to be far more cynical about just what Rose might have done. One, a former White House aide who considers her a dear friend, was asked what he thought when he first read about the gap.

"My first thought," he said, "was that I hoped my secretary would be that loyal."

The women in the office have seen little of Rose Woods but her extraordinary stenographic skills, but the men have seen her function as an almost legendarily firm Nixon appendage. Following Nixon's 1960 defeat, several Republican leaders claimed that Miss Woods had kept them from communicating with the candidate during the election. Senator Styles Bridges, who was chairman of the Senate Republican Policy Committee, telephoned at the end of the campaign, and, as the late columnist George Dixon reported at the time, reached Miss Woods.

"The Vice-President is very busy," she told him.

"I just want to tell him," Bridges said, "that our reports show your boss is not doing too well."

"We disagree with you," Miss Woods replied. "Our reports are different."

In 1968, after Nixon was nominated, former Republican National Committee Chairman Leonard Hall made a courtesy call to the candidate to offer congratulations. Hall had been Nixon's campaign manager in 1960, but he had spent the last year working for two Nixon rivals—Governor George Romney and Governor Nelson Rockefeller. Hall got as far as Rose Mary Woods. She listened to him, said she would give Nixon the message, and ended the conversation with a flat "Don't call us, we'll call you."

"Rose is Nixon's memory," says a former White House aide. "She knows who was with him when the chips were down. She reacts purely politically to people. *What have you done for him lately?* During the Watergate hearings, she was complaining about Senator Baker for asking such tough questions, and she said, 'How dare he do that? We went into his district twice to help him.' " Another Washingtonian tells the story of a local Republican politican Miss Woods deliberately kept off the White House party list because she had heard that during the 1968 convention the man had put a picture of Nixon out on his front lawn with a sign reading, "Would you buy a used car from this man?"

After Nixon's defeat in 1960, Miss Woods followed him to Los Angeles, where he ran for, and lost the race for, governor of California, and then to the New York law firm Nixon, Mudge, Rose, Guthrie & Alexander. She lived on East 50th Street, in a cheerful apartment with a paper rose on the front door, and her friends were happy for her because they felt that for the first time she had some balance in her life. She gave dinner parties. She dated frequently. She was able to afford pretty clothes—her evening dresses are elaborate, with ostrich feathers and the like. She went to the theatre. She made new friends.

When prominent Republicans came to New York, they checked in with Rose. When young Republicans came to New York, they went to see her—and every third time, she gave them a few minutes with The Boss. After 1966, when Nixon decided to try again for the Presidency, she and Pat Buchanan, now a White House aide, were the only people on his staff, and she had considerable influence and total control over access to Nixon. But as the 1968 campaign got under way, her power diminished. And immediately after the election, she came up against the President's new chief of staff, H. R. "Bob" Haldeman.

The fight between her and Haldeman was, at its simplest, over office space. It began with his decision not to let her have Evelyn Lincoln's old office, directly connected to the Oval Office, and it went on for months as he tried unsuccessfully to move her out of the White House entirely and into the Executive Office Building across the alley. But, at bottom, the dispute was over something far more substantive: both wanted to control access to the President. They went to the mat, and the President went with Haldeman. "Rose kept saying she didn't want to go to the President with her problems because he was too busy," said Eloise De La O. "Her office was moved, down the hall. Wouldn't you think the President would be aware of it? It seems to me that if all of a sudden my secretary was moved, I'd notice. But she said she didn't want to worry him. She is so loyal." Significantly, Miss Woods never blamed Nixon for choosing Haldeman over her and instead focused her anger solely against the chief of staff.

The politicians and friends who had always counted on Rose as a way to the President's ear found themselves up against the Berlin Wall, and Rose found herself increasingly excluded from the meetings she had expected to be part of. "Suddenly, she never seemed to be there," said one Republican politician. "She was always off typing or something. After the election, I had a meeting with the President. I was waiting outside, and Haldeman came out and said to come in and meet Dr. Kissinger. I went in. Haldeman, Kissinger, and Nixon were there talking, and Bob was making notes. Then they left and the two of us started to talk. I was just telling the President what the mood was in a couple of states I'd been to—nothing confidential—when Nixon pushed a buzzer. Something I'd said had triggered something in his head. Bob Haldeman came in and took the notes on it on his yellow pad. It struck me not only as a little odd, but also inefficient—he didn't even take shorthand."

In February, 1969, Haldeman managed to keep Miss Woods's name off the list of people who were to accompany the President on his first official trip to Europe, and she was devastated. "It was a classic example of Haldeman's sadism," said one former aide. "She never complained and never raised an objection. But a few days before the trip, the President was leaving the White House and Haldeman walked him out to the helicopter. Nixon must have mentioned something about it, because Haldeman came back to tell Rose that she was going on the trip after all. It was a great victory, although she hadn't done anything." And in 1971, Haldeman and John Ehrlichman made yet another attempt to remove Miss Woods from power. At that point, she was demoralized; she was almost the only old-time Nixon aide who had survived Haldeman's machinations. "Hans and Fritz said she was drinking," said one observer, "and that it had undermined her health. They went to work and started telling Nixon that she was unreliable. Of course, it was their sadistic pressure that had driven her to it. But she pulled herself together and snapped out of it."

"There was a natural clash between Haldeman's zero defects system and Rose's theory that life was more complicated," said another observer. "Haldeman wanted a zero defects system to avoid mistakes, and Rose had the natural insight that that was the way to have a mega-mistake. She provided ways and means of access, and he resented it."

Rose Woods's office is two from the Oval Office, and there she has a staff of three secretaries who handle high-level clerical tasks. The Christmas card list. Letters to the President's friends and supporters. Requests from V.I.P.s. Miss Woods—who is paid $36,000 a year —has continued to perform her customary duties for the President. She is in the office every morning by 8:05 and often works well into the evening hours. "Her work is essentially mountains of mail," says Rhyne, "keeping in contact with people who know the President personally, handling indeterminate numbers of phone calls. It drives you nuts to look at the stack of messages on her desk. The President has continued to use her to do exactly what she did before. I can't see any big change in that. He has not cut her loose. But so far as I know, they've had only one conversation about the tape—on November 14—and nobody has broached the subject with her since. It seems the guy is so intent on what he's doing he doesn't concern himself with anything else. This is a very interesting aspect of the picture."

Miss Woods has always typed most of the President's speeches—and not just his drafts, but the speechwriters' drafts. "I've seen her edit mistakes out of copy that would have gotten everyone in trouble," said one of those speechwriters. "She is also something of an artist. You know how e e cummings writes poetry? She takes a draft of a speech and does a similar thing to it, breaks it up into phrases on the page, makes it much more easy to read, and, incidentally, makes it almost impossible to put back together as prose." Miss Woods also controls the lists for White House parties and prayer breakfasts—which gives her a great deal more power over patronage than might be supposed. And she has functioned as a sort of White House ombudsman, listening sympathetically to complaints from other employees who hope she will go to the President with them. When she goes out at night, she is constantly cornered by Nixon supporters who press letters to the President upon her, ask her to give him messages, give her something they've clipped for him.

Her apartment at the Watergate is a two-bedroom cooperative, furnished by a decorator in beige and brown, and trimmed with some of the mementos she has picked up on her trips with the President—elephants from every country she has been to, a chest from China, an ikon from Spain. There are also lots of flowers—friends have been sending them lately—and they have also been sending posters of a cat hanging from a tree limb, with a printed message: "Hang in there, Baby." She reportedly has enough of them to wallpaper a room.

Rose Mary Woods is hanging in, but her friends say it has been difficult. "Of course she's depressed," says a New York friend, Claudia Val. "Anyone would be, under the circumstances." She is not speaking to Leonard Garment and J. Fred Buzhardt, and apparently a number of people in the White House are not speaking to her. Recently, she called her dear friend Miss De La O, and asked, half-humorously and half-bitterly, "Are *you* still speaking to me?" The antipathy she has always felt for the press has increased; she is not used to being in the public print, even less used to hostile questions from reporters. A few months ago, Miss Woods stood up at a dinner party to toast the President as "the most honest man I have ever known," and reporters continually badger her with the remark. After one of her recent court appearances, a journalist asked her if she would stand by the statement, and Miss Woods lost her temper. "That is a rude, impertinent . . ." she replied. "The answer is yes." Hill & Knowlton executive Gray has tried—strictly in a private capacity—to make sure she goes to a lot of parties and keeps busy, and he also made certain she bought a Christmas tree this year. "This wasn't the year for her not to have one," he said.

Until mid-November, Rose Mary Woods's troubles were not particularly serious; or if they were, she at least felt she was being taken care of by the family. Haldeman was gone, and she had been named executive assistant to the President. She had been asked to give a deposition in the Common Cause lawsuit. (She had sole possession of the secret list of corporate donors to the 1972 campaign—the list is known as "Rosemary's baby"—and used it for party invitations.) The Watergate committee was thinking of subpoenaing her because of her knowledge of the Howard Hughes $100,000 contribution, but had not gotten around to it. There was the milk case, and the fact that she has had a peripheral involvement in the President's murky finances—in 1968 he gave her stock options he held in a Florida land deal, and she doubled her money. But her problems were the President's problems. And then, on November 14, the White House lawyers sat down to play the tape and found the buzz. They could not duplicate it—and they entered Miss Woods's office without her permission in an attempt to reproduce it.

Miss Woods's version of her role in the mystery of

the buzz is as follows. On September 28, the President asked her to go to Camp David for the weekend to transcribe the tapes. She canceled her plans, and on Saturday morning she and the President's appointments secretary, Steve Bull, went up to Dogwood Cabin, and Bull began marking which sections of the tapes Miss Woods was to transcribe. At 10:10 a.m.—apparently in response to a question from Bull—General Haig called and explained to Miss Woods that the subpoena of the June 20 tape covered only the conversation between the President and John Ehrlichman and that she should not bother listening to the one between the President and Haldeman. Miss Woods sat down to work, but she had a difficult time: the quality of the tape was bad and the Sony tape recorder she was using was cumbersome. Saturday afternoon, President Nixon came into the cabin, jiggled the tape back and forth several times, and said he didn't know how she could hear anything on it. Miss Woods worked until 3 a.m. Sunday morning, and got up three hours later to work until 5 p.m., when she joined the Nixons for dinner. "It is one of the few [Sundays] in my life I did not attend Mass," Miss Woods testified, "because I was trying to finish this job."

On Monday, October 1, she resumed work on the June 20 tape back at the White House. Technical Services brought her a Uher 5000 tape recorder they had purchased that day. Sometime around 2 p.m., she was listening to the beginning of the Haldeman conversation—just to verify that Ehrlichman had left the room, she says. The telephone rang. When she got off the phone—four to five minutes later—she realized she had pushed the record button down. She put the tape into reverse and heard the buzz. As soon as she saw the President was alone, she went into his office, the Oval Office, and told him she had made a mistake. "He said there is no problem," Miss Woods testified, "because that is not a subpoenaed tape."

Miss Woods's version continues. In early November,

she was told she would be testifying before Sirica, and on November 7, she met with White House lawyers Leonard Garment and Sam Powers—who have said they did not know about the accident at that point. They told her to answer the questions yes and no, and not to volunteer anything. Miss Woods does not remember being so instructed, but she says it was her impression that her testimony was to cover only the subpoenaed tapes. She appeared in court November 8, and she calmly and deftly told the story of the weekend at Camp David, described at some length how difficult a job it was, and said she had worked on a conversation that seemed to her to be "two to three hours" long "between the President and Ehrlichman, chiefly, and Haldeman, briefly." She added: "It was a very full tape, frankly."

"Were there any precautions taken to assure you would not accidentally hit the erase button?" prosecutor Jill Wine Volner asked.

"Everybody said be terribly careful," Miss Woods replied. "I mean, I don't think I want this to sound like I am bragging, but I don't believe I am so stupid that they had to go over it. . . . I was told if you push that button it will erase, and I do know even on a small machine you can dictate over something and that removes it and I think I used every possible precaution not to do that."

"What special precaution did you take? . . ." Mrs. Volner asked.

"What precautions?" Miss Woods replied. "I used my head. It is the only one I had to use."

From November 26 through 28, Miss Woods appeared once again before Sirica, this time represented by Charles Rhyne, and she finally told the story about the accident and posed for a series of ridiculous pictures at her desk. Judge Sirica asked her why she had not mentioned the accident when she first appeared in court.

"I would say, Your Honor," she replied, "that I

would today, but I didn't then. I think, if you may remember, that I was petrified; it was my first time ever in a courtroom, and I understood that we were talking only about the subpoenaed tapes. And I think all I can say is that I am just dreadfully sorry."

A few questions: How did the President know off the top of his head that that part of the tape was not subpoenaed unless he was already concerned about it? Why did Technical Services buy a new Uher when they had four identical models sitting in the basement not in use? Why did Miss Woods have to listen ahead to make sure Ehrlichman had left the room if Steve Bull had marked the part of the tape she was to transcribe? Why did the White House legal staff think the Haldeman conversation was not subpoenaed when the language of the August 13 revision of the subpoena read: "Respondent met with John Ehrlichman and H. R. Haldeman in his old Executive Office Building office on June 20, 1972, from 10:30 a.m. until approximately 12:45 p.m."? Why did Miss Woods mention that she had worked on "Ehrlichman, chiefly, and Haldeman, briefly" if she did not believe the Haldeman section was covered? How could it have taken her thirty-plus hours at Camp David to transcribe only an hour of conversation—and why did she originally think the conversation was "two or three hours long"? Why did she claim to have the Uher for several hours before the accident when she had had it for only an hour? Why did she think she went in to see the President alone in the Oval Office when White House logs show that on October 1 she saw the President in his Executive Office Building office while he was with his doctor?

In an article in the *New Republic,* Walter Pincus suggests that Miss Woods was telling the truth November 8, and invented the story of the accident some time later. "But in so doing," Pincus writes, "she had no intention of taking the blame for the entire . . .

gap." That is possible. It is also possible that Miss Woods heard the Haldeman section of the tape, knew it was damaging, and erased it deliberately. It is possible she erased the entire eighteen and a half minutes accidentally. It is possible she erased the initial four minutes accidentally and then someone who hoped to stick her with it erased the rest. It is possible that the erasure was already on the tape and Miss Woods was deluded into thinking she had done it. It is possible that the President—or someone working on his behalf —erased the tape and Miss Woods agreed to take part of the blame, never dreaming she would be sold out by the White House legal staff. It is even possible that the experts are wrong in saying that the gap was caused by five to nine separate and deliberate erasures; a faulty diode may have done it. At this point, no one knows—and it is possible that, like many other aspects of the whole Watergate mess, no one will ever know.

And in the meantime, we are left with Rose Mary Woods. The loyal secretary who did it for The Boss? Or the loyal secretary who was set up? The tiger or the lady?

"I was thinking about her last night," Eloise De La O was saying. "Here all these things are happening and there isn't a thing any of us can do for her. It's a maze of things you just can't figure out. I don't know how she's going to get out of it. But I pray for her. And I know she's praying very hard."

March, 1974

No, But I Read the Book

I suppose it is completely presumptuous for me to write even one word on the saga of Pat and Bill and Lance and Kevin and Grant and Delilah and Michele Loud. Last year, I managed to miss every single episode of *An American Family*. But I did catch the Louds on the talk shows, and it seemed to me at the time that, with the possible exception of Tiny Tim, no group of people had ever passed so quickly from being celebrities to being freaks. I was amazed at the amount of time they lingered on, being analyzed in print, taking up space on the air, stealing valuable time from any number of people I would prefer to have read about or seen, even including Shecky Greene. Finally, though, like a toothache, the Louds went away. And the other day, when Pat Loud's book arrived in the mail, I felt terrible that I had not spent the months of their absence grateful for it; it is always easier to have a toothache return when you have at least had the sense to appreciate how wonderful it was not to have had one.

Pat Loud: A Woman's Story was written by Mrs. Loud with Nora Johnson, and the publicity director at Coward, McCann & Geoghegan assures me that its style—which is slick and show-biz rat-a-tat-tat—reflects Mrs. Loud's way of speaking exactly. "Gloria was a lamb chop." "Rose gardens he doesn't walk through." Like that. The book itself is sad and awful, and at times quite fascinating and moving. All these adjectives ring a bell: it seems to me that they were applied to the television series as well. In fact, the only thing about Pat Loud's book that is different from the television series that propelled her into her book contract is that no one who reads it will ever wonder Why She Did It. She did it because she wanted to tell her side. She did it because she had very little else to do. And she did it because she has come to believe that her brand of letting-it-all-hang-out candor is valuable to others in her position. Will she ever learn?

"Every other writer and cocktail circuit sociologist is contemplating the problem of the 46-year-old mother-housewife who suddenly isn't needed anymore," Mrs. Loud writes. "But most of these 'problem women' never had what has saved me, at least so far, from that devastating moment of truth: instant fame." The television show may not have saved Pat Loud from the truth—her own head seems to have done that job perfectly well. But the experience certainly confused her, and confused the issues involved to boot. Pat Loud's book is not the straight I-found-myself-through-divorce women's lib confessional; her case is too unusual. Rather, it is a rambling, perplexing, contradictory account by a woman who is trying, and failing, to make some sense out of a series of events that probably defy sensible explanation.

The real story of the Loud marriage, as told in this book, is a good deal more complicated and tacky, mainly tacky, than what I gather came out in the television series. The Louds and their five children lived in Santa Barbara, California, Pat working hard at being Supermom, Bill at his strip-mining-equipment business. As the marriage went on and the number of children increased, Mrs. Loud began finding telltale clues around the house. First a love letter to Bill from another woman, then a loose glove in his suitcase, lipstick on his handkerchiefs, a brochure from a Las Vegas hotel. The love letter enraged her so that she packed her four children into the family car—she was pregnant with her fifth—and drove off into the night. As it turned out, she did not get very far; Mrs. Loud, who has no selectivity index whatsoever, explains: "When I'm pregnant, I have the trots all the time, and sometimes it's really essential to get to a john fast . . . and there wasn't any gas station. . . . So finally I turned around and went home." In 1966, she found a set of her husband's cuff links, engraved "To Bill, Eternally Yours, Kitty," and all hell broke loose. Her husband assured her he had bought the cuff links in a pawn shop, but she did not believe him. So she snuck off, had an extra set of his office keys made, and while he was off on a business trip she went to look through his files.

"It was all there," she writes, "as though it had been waiting for me for years—credit card slips telling of restaurants I'd never been to and hotels I'd never stayed at, plane tickets to places I'd never seen, even pictures of Bill and his girls as they grinned and screwed their way around the countryside."

Bill Loud returned from his business trip. Pat Loud slugged him, in front of the children. He slugged her back, in front of the children. They both went to see a psychiatrist. They both stopped seeing the psychiatrist. They spent night after night getting drunk as Bill Loud recited the intimate sexual details of his infidelities. The subject of open marriage was introduced. Pat Loud began going to local bars during lunch and picking up businessmen. "We would have a few drinks and some tortillas," she recalls. "Then we would let nature take its course." She threatened divorce. He started seeing his women again. And in the midst of this idyllic existence, Craig Gilbert, a film-maker with a contract from public television, came into their home and told them he was looking for "an attractive, articulate California family" to do a one-hour special about.

It is impossible to read this book and not suspect that Craig Gilbert knew exactly what he was doing when he picked the Louds, knew after ten minutes with them and the clinking ice in their drinks that he had found the perfect family to show exactly what he must have intended to show all along—the emptiness of American family life. Occasionally, in the course of this book, Pat Loud starts to suspect this, nibbles around it, yaps like a puppy at the ankles of truth, then tosses the idea aside in favor of loftier philosophical pronouncements. "If he knew it," she concludes, "it was not necessarily because he actively smelled it about us, but because he knew in a way what we didn't—that life is lousy and it's tragic and it's supposed to be and you can pretend otherwise if you want, but if you do, you're wrong."

Gilbert had no trouble persuading the Louds to cooperate. Bill had always been outgoing and exhibitionistic. Pat, for her part, saw the show as a way to appear as she had always wanted to—the perfect mother, cheerfully beating egg whites in her copper bowls. When Gilbert informed them that the show was going to be so good that he would shoot enough for five specials and then twelve, the Louds consented, apparently without a tremor of anxiety.

"Of course," Pat Loud writes, "if you're going to be in print or on the radio or TV, you can't help thinking of all the people who will read or see you, and the first ones I thought of were all Bill's women. There they would sit in frowzy little rented rooms scattered about California, Oregon, Washington, and Arizona, little gifts from Bill here and there, a memento from some trip or something he'd bought them, pathetic scraps of forgotten pleasure in their failed and lonely worlds. Their bleached blond hair would be falling sloppily out of its hairpins and their enormous breasts would be falling equally sloppily out of their torn, spotty negligees as they clutched their glasses of Scotch and rested their fat ankles on footstools to relieve their aching, varicose veins. . . . In pathetic, panting interest they would turn on their televisions to look at the

Louds, and they would weep. . . . If they'd had Bill for a few hours or days, if they'd had a few sessions of what they probably thought of as blinding ecstasy, I had had him a thousand times more."

Pat Loud offers a number of other explanations as to why her family agreed to Gilbert's proposal—the one she seems to believe most firmly is that anyone would have. But she is less sure about why the reaction to the show was so enormous. "What nerve have we touched?" she asks at one point. "I would like to know; I would really like to know." I suspect I know. I think the American public has an almost insatiable need to feel superior to people who appear to have everything, and the Louds were the perfect vehicle to fill that need. There they were, a beautiful family with a beautiful house with a beautiful pool, and one son was a homosexual, the rest of the children lolled about, uninterested in anything, and the marriage was breaking up. All of it was on television, in *cinéma vérité*—a medium that at its best (I'm thinking of the Maysleses' *Salesman* and the Canadian Film Board's *Lonely Boy* and *The Most*) has always tended to specialize in a certain amount of implicit condescension.

It is on the subject of the making of the series that Pat Loud is most interesting. *Cinéma vérité* film-makers have always insisted that after a time, their subjects forget the cameras are there, but as Pat Loud makes clear, it's just not possible. "You can't forget the camera," she writes, "and everybody's instinct is to try and look as good as possible for it, all the time, and to keep kind of snapping along being active, eager, cheery, and productive. Out go those moments when you're just in a kind of nothing period. . . . You don't realize how many of those you have until you're trying not to have them. . . . And what you also don't realize is that you *have* to have them—they're like REM sleep."

Ultimately, Pat Loud seems to have come to believe

that she owed more to the film-makers than she did to herself or her husband; any concept of dignity or privacy she may have had evaporated in the face of pressure from them. Again she nibbles around the edges of this, almost but not quite getting it, but the suggestions of what happened are there: the illiterate Californians trying to impress the erudite Easterners; the boring, slothful family attempting to come up with a dramatic episode to justify all that footage; the woman who had always tried to please men—first her father, then her husband—now transferring it all to Craig Gilbert.

And when, in the course of events, Pat Loud decided she wanted a divorce, Craig Gilbert convinced her that she owed it to him, to all of them, to do it on the air. "If I decided to divorce during the filming," Mrs. Loud says Gilbert told her, "I must be honest enough to do it openly and not confuse the issue further by refusing to allow it to be shot." Again she almost has it, almost sees how she was conned, and then falls into utter nonsense. "Couldn't it be," she asks, "that since circumstance and fate had put me in a position to rip away the curtain of hypocrisy, that maybe, just maybe, we could help other families face their problems more honestly?" And then she switches gears, and makes sense again: "A psychiatrist told a friend of mine recently that in his experience he'd found that there is almost always a third force present when divorce finally happens. The miserable marriage can wobble on for years on end, until something or somebody comes along and pushes one of the people over the brink. . . . It's usually another man . . . or another woman . . . or possibly a supportive psychiatrist; in my case, it was a whole production staff and a camera crew. . . ."

And so the marriage and the television series ended, and along came the notoriety. And now there is the book, and there will be more: more talk shows, more interviews. It all seems sad; there is no way to read this book and not feel that this bumbling woman is way over her head. She has made a fool of herself on television, and now she is making a fool of herself in print. She does not understand that it is just as hard to be honest successfully as it is to lie successfully. And now, God help her, she has moved to New York. She will get a job, she tells us at the end of the book, and perhaps she will be able to fulfill her fantasy. Here is Pat Loud's last fantasy. She's at this swell New York cocktail party, "exchanging terribly New York in-type gossip about who's backing what new play and who got how much for the paperback rights to Philip Roth's latest," and there is this man who takes her to dinner, and then to bed, and they have a wonderful affair. "I'm not saying he would solve everything, or pick up the pieces, or even make me happy. Nor is he as important as a good job. But the nice thing about fantasies is that you don't have to explain them to anybody. They are absolutely free." There she goes again, almost making sense, talking about the importance of work, and the need not to look to anyone for the solution of her problems, and then she blows it all. "They are absolutely free." That's the thing about fantasies. They're not absolutely free. Sometimes you pay dearly for them. Which is something Pat Loud ought to have learned by now. Will she ever?

March, 1974

Crazy Ladies: II

It was, as these things go, a fairly ordinary week. One Flying Wallenda. Two midgets who claimed to be the world's smallest married couple. An anthropologist who insisted that people who eat bear meat become more aggressive than people who eat eggs. A tiger who chewed up the carpet. And the requisite number of folk singers, politicians, writers, actors, doctors, palm readers, and tax experts who travel the country filling up the air time on local television talk shows. Not that any of them mattered to me. The reason I was there—and the reason a great many more people than usual watched *The Panorama Show* in Washington the week of April 1—was that Martha Mitchell was the co-host. Martha of the late-night phone calls, Martha the black-and-blue political prisoner, Martha who lives alone now while her husband commutes between his Essex House suite and his trial in the federal courthouse, Martha whose own daughter has chosen to spend most of her time with her father—Martha was making her first public appearance since "the mess," as she refers to it, began. From Monday through Friday, she sat under the lights, doing a perfectly creditable job, and I sat there in the studio watching and waiting—I'm not sure for what. A few bitchy remarks about Richard Nixon, maybe. A couple of tidbits about her own state of mind. An insight or two about political wives, or about how-the-mighty-have-fallen, or some such. I had never confused Martha Mitchell with Diogenes, never thought she knew a

great deal about Watergate, never found her anything
but a rather frowzy, excessive, blathering woman who
never (until the Watergate break-in) said anything that
I found remotely sympathetic. I did not expect to find
her charming, and I did not expect to find her canny,
and I certainly did not expect to find her moving. All of
which she was. At the end of the week, one reporter
who covered the show suggested in print that the staff
of *Panorama* had taken advantage of Martha, had used
her, had held her up as a freak, had titillated the public
with coy and tasteless references to her sanity. It
seemed to me more complicated than that. Martha
Mitchell has always used the media at least as well
as they have used her. She even told a story about it
on the show. She was asked by host Maury Povich
about her late-night phone calls to the press.

"A lot of them were planned," she explained. "I'd
call in the daytime and say, 'Now this is my story, let's
put it out at midnight.' Sometimes they'd ask where
I was calling from, and I'd say the balcony of Watergate. Now it's not in any way possible to get a telephone out on the balcony of Watergate, but that was
just a little come-on to make it more interesting."

"You mean you could determine when a story would
be broken?" Povich asked.

"Well," she said, "I learned pretty early on in the
game what you have to do to get a story on the wires
or printed. That's what I did."

"I thought it was all off the top of your head," said
Povich.

"Well," said Martha Mitchell, "I try to be dumb."

The Panorama Show got exactly what it wanted
from Martha Mitchell—a lot of publicity and attention.
And she got from it the chance to prove that she wasn't
crazy. In the end, it was a fair trade.

It is, of course, extremely easy to become known in
Washington as a crazy lady. Even Marion Javits is
thought of there as a crazy lady. But Martha Mitchell's
reputation as one was earned. She always reveled in

the image she created as the slightly dizzy dame whose husband could not control her. In fact, she rarely said anything he did not approve of; nonetheless, the image worked perfectly. But in June, 1972, it all caught up with her. No one ever takes crazy ladies seriously. And so when she called U.P.I.'s Helen Thomas to claim that she was being held prisoner in a California motel and injected with drugs against her will, the press dutifully reported the claim and did virtually nothing to check it out. She was telling the truth—but almost no one knows that, even now. It is almost impossible to think of another politician's wife who could have gone through such an experience and had so little serious attention paid to it. When John Mitchell resigned as the President's campaign manager shortly afterward, the White House had an easy time convincing the press —and the public—that he had done so in order to look after his wife. Now, almost two years later, the Mitchells are separated; he is facing an apparently endless series of court battles; and she is living alone in a Fifth Avenue cooperative where—she notes sadly —she has never even had a chance to use the dining room.

Mrs. Mitchell's appearance on *Panorama* was negotiated by the show's producer, Jane Henry Caper, through a mutual friend; she was paid just above the $480 AFTRA scale. There were no explicit ground rules set for the appearance, but Povich, the host of the show, deliberately stayed away from any direct questions about John Mitchell and his legal difficulties, and he waited until midweek to ask her directly about her own problems. He need not have waited. Martha Mitchell may not be a brilliant woman, but her instincts are first-rate; she knew exactly when to laugh off a question and when to take the opening to make a point about herself.

At the beginning of the week, though, it seemed likely that Mrs. Mitchell would provide only indirect hints about her state of mind. She did get off a couple of zingers at the President—particularly when she told of converting her husband to Republicanism. "The day I talked my husband out of calling the President Tricky Dick, I could shoot myself," she said. But the most interesting moment on Monday's show came when she turned to Helen Gahagan Douglas, who ran unsuccessfully for the Senate against Richard Nixon in 1950. "Well, Helen," she said, "I want to ask you something. I think you went through a certain smear campaign in those years. How do you overcome a smear campaign? How do you explain it to your children?" It was a wonderful question; unfortunately, Mrs. Douglas did not answer it, and the show went on to far more mundane things—including an extended series of misunderstandings between the two women. As Diana McLellan put it in the Washington *Star*, Mrs. Douglas and Mrs. Mitchell "hit it off immediately, in the splendid way of two very polite women, each of whom insists on believing that the other is in total agreement with her, no matter how diametrically opposed she is."

"What worries you as you walk around?" Mrs. Douglas asked Mrs. Mitchell. "What do you see that distresses you?"

"I have got to the point, Helen, where I can't read the papers," replied Martha. "Everything worries me. What worries me more than anything is the example this country is setting for the younger people."

"That's true," Mrs. Douglas grimly agreed, apparently thinking Mrs. Mitchell was referring to the Nixon Administration.

"For instance," Martha went on, "this streaking. I see a TV show the other night and there go nudes in front of me. What is now left? Why should children go out and streak?"

The subject of streaking came up with some frequency during the week, and Martha continued to be baffled by it. "Where did it start?" she asked. "At one of the Ivy League colleges?" It was a perfect subject for her: one of her gifts as a co-host is that except when she wants to make a point about herself, she asks exactly the kinds of unsophisticated questions any Middle American housewife would, and has absolutely no embarrassment about revealing how naïve she is. "This conversation is too technical for me," she sighed during what was in fact a rather technical explanation of tax shelters. "I'm not sure what you're explaining," she said to two housing officials who had been totally unintelligible for fifteen minutes. "What does this mean?" she asked after reading a completely meaningless weather report. "Is it going to rain or isn't it?"

The first reference to her mental health came up on Wednesday—and she chose to take it lightly. Pat Loud was on the show, and she remarked that since moving to New York she had seen more crazy people than she ever had in her life.

"Don't you think that's because American people have too much leisure?" asked Martha.

"No," said Pat Loud. "I don't think so."

Povich turned to Mrs. Mitchell. "I don't know whether I should, but I will bring this subject up," he said. "There were nasty rumors about you, Martha, when you left Washington, in this circumstance, and I was wondering how you lived with that."

"Well," said Martha, "don't you see, I'm still crazy. It doesn't take very long to find that out. But, you know, I'm happy. They say that crazy people are happier than anyone else. Look at me."

On Thursday, Helen Thomas and *Time* magazine's Bonnie Angelo came on as guests—and Martha, surrounded by the closest thing she has to friends these days, relaxed. Povich fumbled in with a question—this time to Miss Thomas—about Martha's sanity, and Martha listened as Miss Thomas defended her. "Martha Mitchell hit this town like a bombshell," she recalled, and as she talked, Martha Mitchell seemed to become sadder—which was understandable, since Helen Thomas sounded a little as if she were talking about a dead person. Povich asked how the telephone connection between the two of them began. "You know, it always amazes me," said Martha. "Why am I associated with a telephone when we've had two Presidents of late who've done nothing but telephone all night long? I mean, why should they pick on a poor woman? Look at Johnson. Look at Richard Nixon. I have more funny stories to tell about Richard Nixon telephoning the apartment at two or three in the morning, and I'm going to tell them sometime."

"How about right now?" said Bonnie Angelo.

"No," said Martha. "I'm saving it for my book."

Miss Angelo asked how Martha felt about the press.

"I want to say, from the bottom of my heart, that I think that I wouldn't be sitting here today if it weren't for the press," she said. "They have literally saved me from an asylum, and from I don't know what. And I can take it one step further. If I hadn't made that telephone call to Helen in California, the people that were behind all this, that were holding me a prisoner, would not have taken into consideration that the press knew that if anything happened to Martha Mitchell, Helen would have been there looking for me. It literally saved my life."

Bonnie Angelo pointed out that the White House planted the rumors about Martha's crack-up and told reporters she was the reason Mitchell resigned.

"Poor John," said Martha. "Poor John had to take care of me." She smiled ruefully and shook her head. "One of the funniest things is, and I say that not meaning funny, but in recent months people in the White House have called my friends and said, 'Why do you listen to Martha Mitchell? She's crazy as a loon. Don't print anything about her.' "

"I want to ask Martha," said Miss Angelo. "Did you enjoy living in the spotlight? Are you happy you had those years as a public figure?"

"I don't think I've had time to get around to that, Bonnie," said Martha Mitchell. "There've been too many hurts to really analyze the situation."

Friday, after her last show, I sat down with Martha Mitchell in the *Panorama* offices at WTTG. A staff member came in to tell her that they had gotten hundreds of phone calls praising her performance. "Isn't that great?" she said. "With all the hell I've been through, to hear a little praise. I've gone through all this by myself, as you know. This has been an extremely trying period for me, from the standpoint of Martha. I've been fighting a one-man battle, and I haven't just been fighting City Hall—I've been fighting the federal government. You must realize that everything that's happened to me has been caused by the cover-up of Watergate. I was hidden, literally, for a long period of time, hidden by them, and also hidden by myself, because I had been so tremendously crushed. When you believe as I believed, and worked as hard as I worked —and nobody in Washington worked as hard as Martha Mitchell—and then all of a sudden to have your world crushed in front of you, which happened to me in California. Why did people call her crazy? Why did people call her an alcoholic? Because they were trying to shut Martha Mitchell up, and they didn't know how to do it.

"I lived for my family. We were the tightest-knit little family you've ever seen. They used to say we had a perfect marriage, a perfect love affair. We did. Every day he used to tell me I was the most wonderful woman in the world. And John always had so much confidence in me. I don't feel I'm a deserted woman. This is not a normal marital breakup. It's much more intricate. Because a man doesn't change in twenty-four hours from thinking his wife is the most wonderful person in the world."

And so Martha Mitchell went off to her hotel. She was spending the weekend in Washington and planned to attend the Counter-Gridiron party. "The busy person is the happy person," she said as she left. Oh, sure. And maybe the crazy person is the happy person, too. But Martha Mitchell is neither busy nor crazy nor happy. There is not much call for yesterday's celebrities. There is probably a lesson in this, something about crazy ladies, or crying wolf, or maybe something about Richard Nixon—but I don't know what it is. To some extent Martha Mitchell got what she deserved. But still . . .

April, 1974

Conundrum

As I suppose everyone knows by now, James Morris was four years old and sitting under the piano listening to his mother play Sibelius when he was seized with the irreversible conviction that he ought to have been born a girl. By the age of nine, he was praying nightly for the miracle. "Let me be a girl. Amen." He went on to the army, became a journalist, climbed Mount Everest with Sir Edmund Hillary, won awards for his books, and had four children with a wife who knew that all he really wanted was a sex change. Almost two years ago, he went off to a clinic in Casablanca that had dirty floors, shaved off his pubic hair, "and went to say goodbye to myself in the mirror. We would never meet again, and I wanted to give that other self a long last look in the eye and a wink of luck." The wink of luck did that other self no good at all: the next morning, it was lopped off, and James Morris woke up to find himself as much a woman as hormones and surgery could make him. He promptly sold his dinner jacket and changed his name.

This entire mess could doubtless have been avoided had James Morris been born an Orthodox Jew (in which case he could have adopted the standard Jewish prayer thanking God for *not* making him a woman) or had he gone to see a good Freudian analyst, who might have realized that any young boy sitting under a piano was probably looking up his mother's skirt. But no such luck. James Morris has become Jan Morris, an Englishwoman who wears sweater sets and pearls, blushes frequently, bursts into tears at the littlest things, and loves having a gossip with someone named Mrs. Weatherby. Mrs. Weatherby, Morris writes, "really is concerned . . . about my migraine yesterday; and when I examine myself I find that I am no less genuinely distressed to hear that Amanda missed the school outing because of her ankle."

Conundrum is Jan Morris's book about her experience, and I read it with a great deal of interest, largely because I always wanted to be a girl, too. I, too, felt that I was born into the wrong body, a body that refused, in spite of every imprecation and exercise I could manage, to become anything but the boyish, lean thing it was. I, too, grew up wishing for protectors, strangers to carry my bags, truck drivers to whistle out windows. I wanted more than anything to be something I will never be—feminine, and feminine in the worst way. Submissive. Dependent. Soft-spoken. Coquettish. I was no good at all at any of it, no good at being a girl; on the other hand, I am not half-bad at being a woman. In contrast, Jan Morris is perfectly awful at being a woman; what she has become instead is exactly what James Morris wanted to become those many years ago. A girl. And worse, a forty-seven-year-old girl. And worst of all, a forty-seven-year-old *Cosmopolitan* girl. To wit:

"So I well understand what Kipling had in mind, about sisters under the skin. Over coffee a lady from Montreal effuses about Bath—'I don't know if you've done any traveling yourself' (not too much, I demurely lie) 'but I do feel it's important, don't you, to see how other people really live.' I bump into Jane W—— in the street, and she tells me about Archie's latest excess—'Honestly, Jan, you don't know how lucky you are.' I buy some typing paper—'How lovely to be able to write, you make me feel a proper dunce'—and walking home again to start work on a new chapter, find that workmen are in the flat, taking down a picture-rail. One of them has knocked my little red horse off the mantelpiece, chipping its enameled rump. I restrain my annoyance, summon a fairly frosty smile, and make them all cups of tea, but I am thinking to myself, as they sheepishly help themselves to sugar, a harsh feminist thought. It would be a man, I think. Well it would, wouldn't it?"

It is a truism of the women's movement that the exaggerated concepts of femininity and masculinity have done their fair share to make a great many people unhappy, but nowhere is this more evident than in Jan Morris's mawkish and embarrassing book. I first read of Morris in a Sunday *New York Times Magazine* article that brought dignity and real sensitivity to Morris's obsession. But Morris's own sensibility is so giddy and relentlessly cheerful that her book has almost no dignity at all. What she has done in it is to retrace his/her life (I am going to go crazy from the pronouns and adjectives here) by applying sentimental gender judgments to everything. Oxford is wonderful because it is feminine. Venice is sublime because it is feminine. Statesmen are dreadful because they are masculine. "Even more than now," Morris writes of his years as a foreign correspondent, "the world of affairs was dominated by men. It was like stepping from cheap theater into reality, to pass from the ludicrous goings-on of minister's office or ambassador's study into the private house behind, where women were to be found doing real things, like bringing up children, painting pictures, or writing home."

And as for sex—but let Morris tell you about men and women and sex. "You are doubtless wondering, especially if you are male, what about sex? . . . One of the genuine and recurrent surprises of my life concerns the importance to men of physical sex. . . . For me the actual performance of the sexual act seemed of secondary importance and interest. I suspect this is true for most women. . . . In the ordinary course of events [the sex act] struck me as slightly distasteful, and I could imagine it only as part of some grand act, a declaration of absolute interdependence, or even a sacrifice."

Over the years, Morris saw a number of doctors, several of whom suggested he try homosexuality. (He had tried it several times before, but found it aesthetically unpleasant.) A meeting was arranged with the owner of a London art gallery. "We had a difficult lunch together," Morris writes, "and he made eyes at the wine waiter over the fruit salad." The remark is interesting, not just because of its hostility toward homosexuals but also because Jan Morris now makes exactly those same sorts of eyes at wine waiters—on page 150 of her book, in fact.

As James turns into a hermaphrodite and then into Jan, the prose in the book, which is cloying enough to begin with, turns into a kind of overembellished, simile-laden verbiage that makes the style of Victorian women novelists seem spare. Exclamation points and italicized words appear with increasing frequency. Everything blushes. James Morris blushes. His "small breasts blossomed like blushes." He starts talking to the flowers and wishing them a Happy Easter. He becomes even more devoted to animals. He is able for the first time ("the scales dropped from my eyes") to look out a plane window and see things on the ground below not as cars and homes seen at a distance but "Lo! . . . as dolls' houses and dinky toys." Shortly before the operation, he and his wife, Elizabeth, whose understanding defies understanding, take a trip, both as women, through Oregon. "How merrily we traveled!" Morris writes. "What fun the Oregonians gave us! How cheerfully we swapped badinage with boatmen and lumberjacks, flirtatious garage hands and hospitable trappers! I never felt so liberated, or more myself, nor was I ever more fond of Elizabeth. 'Come on in, girls,' the motel men would say, and childish though I expect it sounds to you, silly in itself, perhaps a little pathetic, possibly grotesque, still if they had touched me with an accolade of nobility, or clad me ceremonially in crimson, I could not have been more flattered." The only thing Morris neglects to write into this passage is a little face with a smile on it.

Morris is infuriatingly vague about the reactions of her children (she blandly insists they adjusted perfectly) and of Elizabeth (she says they are still the closest of friends). "I am not the first," Morris writes, "to discover that one recipe for an idyllic marriage is a blend of affection, physical potency and sexual incongruity." (Idyllic marriage? Where your husband becomes a lady? I suppose we owe this to creeping Harold-and-Vitaism; still, it is one of the more ridiculous trends of recent years to confuse great friendships with great marriages; great marriages are when you have it all.) As for her new sex life, Jan Morris lyrically trills that her sexuality is now unbounded. But how?

Unfortunately, she is a good deal more explicit about the details of what she refers to as "truly the symptoms of womanhood." "The more I was treated as a woman, the more woman I became," she writes. "I adapted willy-nilly. If I was assumed to be incompetent at reversing cars, or opening bottles, oddly, incompetent I found myself becoming. If a case was thought too heavy for me, inexplicably I found it so myself. . . . I discovered that even now men prefer women to be less informed, less able, less talkative, and certainly less self-centered than they are themselves; so I generally obliged them. . . . I did not particularly want to be good at reversing cars, and did not in the least mind being patronized by illiterate garage-men, if it meant they were going to give me some extra trading stamps. . . . And when the news agent seems to look at me with approval, or the man in the milk-cart smiles, I feel absurdly elated, as though I have been given a good review in the Sunday *Times*. I know it is nonsense, but I cannot help it."

The truth, of course, is that Jan Morris does not know it is nonsense. She thinks that is what it is about.

And I wonder about all this, wonder how anyone in this day and age can think that this is what being a woman is about. And as I wonder, I find myself thinking a harsh feminist thought. It would be a man, I think. Well, it would, wouldn't it?

June, 1974

ABOUT THE AUTHOR

NORA EPHRON lives in Manhattan and writes a column for *Esquire* magazine. Her work has appeared in *New York* magazine, *Rolling Stone, Ms., The New York Times Book Review,* and *The New Yorker.* She is also the author of *Wallflower at the Orgy.*

RELAX!
SIT DOWN
and Catch Up On Your Reading!

☐	BLACK SUNDAY by Thomas Harris	(2100—$1.95)
☐	THE MONEYCHANGERS by Arthur Hailey	(2300—$1.95)
☐	ASPEN by Burt Hirschfeld	(2491—$1.95)
☐	THE EAGLE HAS LANDED by Jack Higgins	(2500—$1.95)
☐	RAGTIME by E. L. Doctorow	(2600—$2.25)
☐	THE ODESSA FILE by Frederick Forsyth	(2964—$1.95)
☐	THE BELL JAR by Sylvia Plath	(6400—$1.75)
☐	DRAGONARD by Rupert Gilchrist	(6452—$1.75)
☐	FAMILY SECRETS by Rona Jaffe	(6464—$1.95)
☐	THE DAY OF THE JACKAL by Frederick Forsyth	(7377—$1.75)
☐	THE HARRARD EXPERIMENT by Robert Rimmer	(7950—$1.50)
☐	THE LOVE MACHINE by Jacqueline Susann	(7970—$1.75)
☐	ONCE IS NOT ENOUGH by Jacqueline Susann	(8000—$1.95)
☐	THE MANNINGS by Fred Mustard Stewart	(8400—$1.95)
☐	BURR by Gore Vidal	(8484—$1.95)
☐	JAWS by Peter Benchley	(8500—$1.95)
☐	TINKER, TAILOR, SOLDIER, SPY by John Le Carre	(8844—$1.95)
☐	THE DOGS OF WAR by Frederick Forsyth	(8884—$1.95)

Buy them at your local bookstore or use this handy coupon for ordering: